WARBIRDTECH SERIES

VOLUME 3

NORTH AMERICAN F-86

SabreJet DAY FIGHTERS

BY KRIS HUGHES AND WALTER DRANEM

specialtypress

PUBLISHERS AND WHOLESALERS

Published by
Specialty Press Publishers and Wholesalers
11481 Kost Dam Road
North Branch, MN 55056
United States of America
(612) 583-3239

Distributed in the UK and Europe by
Airlife Publishing Ltd.
101 Longden Road
Shrewsbury
SY3 9EB
England

ISBN 0-933424-66-3

Designed by Greg Compton

Printed in the United States of America

TABLE OF CONTENTS

THE NORTH AMERICAN F-86 SABREJET DAY FIGHTERS

PREFACE

THE THANKS GO TO—

The North American F-86 SabreJet was the end result of a combined effort of many fine people both at North American Aviation and within the United States Army Air Force and United States Air Force. Similarly, this book is a combined effort of two authors based on many, many interviews with personnel from North American and the US Air Force, without whose help this effort would never have succeeded.

Special thanks have to go to three fine gentlemen from North American Aviation and Rockwell International. First is Mr. Gene Boswell, the Public Relations Manager at North American as far back as anyone can remember. Gene opened the North American archives up and worked diligently in obtaining the necessary photographs, many of which have never been seen before.

Second is Mr. John Henderson, a retired North American Tech Rep with the F-86 project from the late 1940s to the end of the active program. John offered much insight into Sabre equipment and maintenance, especially during the Korean War. Third is Mr. Ed Horkey, one of

Four different F-86As on the ramp at Johnson AB, Japan in early 1951. With the Chinese ready to overrun the base at Kimpo, the 4th FIG hastily left on January 2nd 1951, taking their F-86As to Johnson AB. From Johnson, the Sabres could no longer reach the area in northwest Korea where the MiGs were based, i.e. "MiG Alley." They returned to Korea in February 1951, first at Taegu, then flying air to air missions in MiG Alley from Suwon. (Brig. Gen. Alonzo Walter)

Capt. Martin Johansen flew this 335th FS F-86A as part of a two ship demonstration for the 1949 National Air Races held at Cleveland Municipal Airport. The aircraft carries the indian head marking of the 335th FS. The squadrons of the 4th FG were also transferred to Air Defense Command in January 1950 and redesignated fighter interceptor units. (Warren Bodie)

the key engineers on the F-86 from the beginning. Ed lent his considerable memory of the earliest XP-86 programs, as well as the initial flight test data. Both John and Ed proofread various sections to make the book as accurate as possible.

Special mention has to go to the F-86 Sabre Pilots Association, whose members lent their valuable memories and photos for the project. A special thanks should go to Dee Harper, President of the Sabre Pilots, for all the help he provided in moving the members to help with the project.

To the staff, both present or past, of the United States Air Force Museum, go a lot of kudos for loaning of photos, manuals, classified and de-classified documents over the years. The USAFM is a great place to visit, and an even better place to do research on any aircraft flown by the US Air Force. The best part is, the airplanes are right there on display.

Last but not least, a special thanks go to Mr. SabreJet, Larry Davis, Editor of *SabreJet Classics*, for opening his vast files on the Sabre to the authors. All we had to do was

call him on the phone and ask for it. If he had it, and it was rare that he didn't, he would have it in the mail to us within days.

Thanks to everyone else that may have lent support, either materialistic of otherwise.

KRIS HUGHES AND WALTER DRANEM
1996

This book is dedicated to the men that built the Sabre, maintained the Sabre, and flew the Sabre.

We salute you!

BIRTH OF THE SABRE

In 1939, the first operational airplane powered by a gas turbine engine was built. All previous powered airplanes had either an inline or radial internal combustion engine, using either gasoline or diesel for fuel, and driving a propeller. Very simply, the gas turbine used its exhaust gas as power, commonly called thrust. In Nazi Germany, Ernst Heinkel had installed a gas turbine engine in his He-178 airframe, making its first flight on 27 August 1939. Across the Channel in England, British engineer Frank Whittle had one of his new gas turbines installed in a Gloster G-40 airframe. These two aircraft would ultimately lead to an entirely new concept which would revolutionize the aviation world—the jet aircraft.

In the US, little concern was paid to the new powerplant. The War Department was busy simply trying to catch up with the rest of the world regarding "normal" airplane types. There was a war in Europe, and another heating up in the Pacific. And the US was far behind all the nations already involved with regards to high performance aircraft. It wouldn't be until the development of the Lockheed P-38 and Republic P-47, that the US could expend money and energy on frivolous things like gas turbines and jet aircraft.

When the P-51 Mustang (considered the best fighter built in World War Two) was developed, the Germans already had an operational jet fighter ready to take on the Allies—the Messerschmitt Me-262. The Me-262 was flying and ready for operations as early as 1943. Only stupidity on Hitler's part, and luck by the Allies, kept the German jets from decimating the Allied bomber forces as the Me-262 was a full 150 MPH faster than any propeller-driven airplane flying.

The only known photo of the XP-86 straight wing design at mock-up, which was unveiled at Inglewood in June 1945. Only the left side of the mock-up was finished and inspected on June 20th 1945. Although the XP-86 never went beyond the mock-up stage, its Navy cousin, the XFJ-1 Fury went into full production, becoming the first operational jet fighter for the Navy. (NAA)

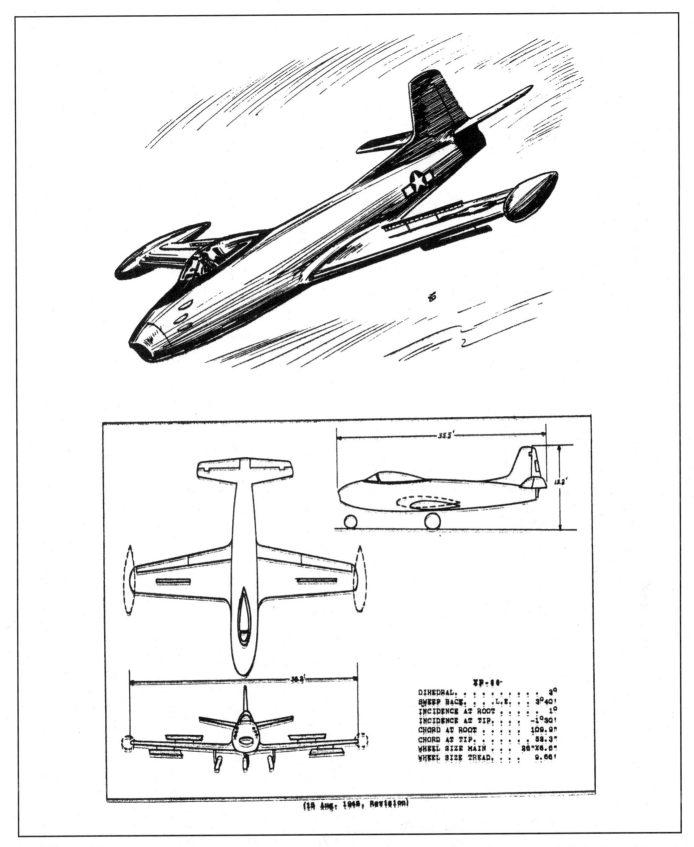

North American Aviation drawings showing the original design, layout and specifications of the XP-86 as of August 15th 1945. The design was changed to that of a swept winged aircraft in a couple of months. Note the basic wing and tail planforms are that of a P-51D Mustang, and the air brakes above and below the wings are derived from another Mustang variant, the A-36A Invader.

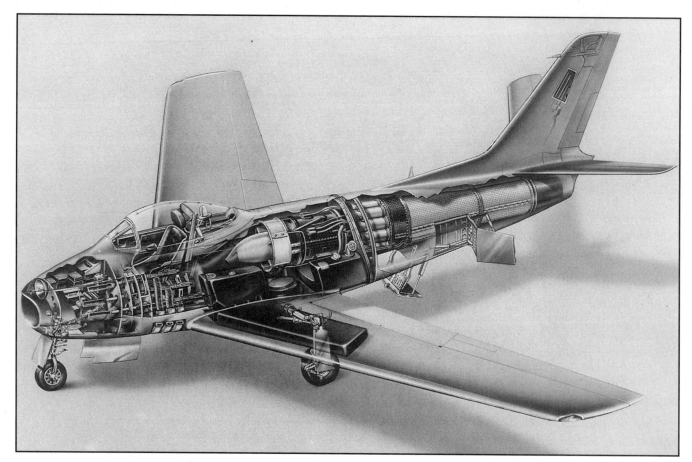

This artists rendering of the XP-86 swept wing design shows many items that eventually were deleted or changed on production airplanes. Note how the dive brakes on the rear fuselage sides are hinged at the rear, and the actuating arms are behind the dive brake panel. On production airplanes, the brakes were hinged at the front. This rendering also clearly shows the underfuselage dive brake door, which was deleted entirely. (NAA)

By 1942, a few US companies were becoming intrigued by the gas turbine. With engines borrowed from Whittle, Bell Aircraft Company unveiled the XP-59A Airacomet in October 1942. But its performance wasn't even on a par with contemporary prop fighter types. Lockheed built the XP-80 powered by a DeHavilland Goblin turbine, making its first flight on January 8, 1944. Although the XP-80 broke the 500 MPH barrier, it still was not competitive with German jets. Republic's XP-84 promised still greater performance, but it wouldn't fly until 1946.

On November 22, 1944, NAA initiated a design study (RD-1265) for a jet fighter proposal. The design was straight forward in all respects, and used a lot of P-51 technology. It was just powered by a gas turbine. The flying surfaces, the wings and tail, were very similar to those found on the latest P-51. The wing was of the latest laminar flow design, with straight leading and trailing edges. There were no "devices" added to the wings to either smooth air flow or increase lift.

The fuselage was short, rotund, and very smooth. The nose was open to induct air to the TG 180 gas turbine engine. The TG 180 was a General Electric license-built version of the DeHavilland Goblin gas turbine. The main problem was that the project (NA-134) was designed FOR THE NAVY. The Navy promptly ordered three prototypes of the NA-134 on 1 January 1945.

The US Army Air Force got interested in the North American Navy jet project in the Spring of 1945. On May 18, 1945, NAA received a letter contract to build three prototype aircraft for the Army, with the designation XP-86. The General Operational Requirements called for a day fighter of medium range, that could operate in both escort and fighter-bomber missions, with a top speed above 600 MPH. This last item in the GOR was considered by many to be outside the scope of any jet designs at the time.

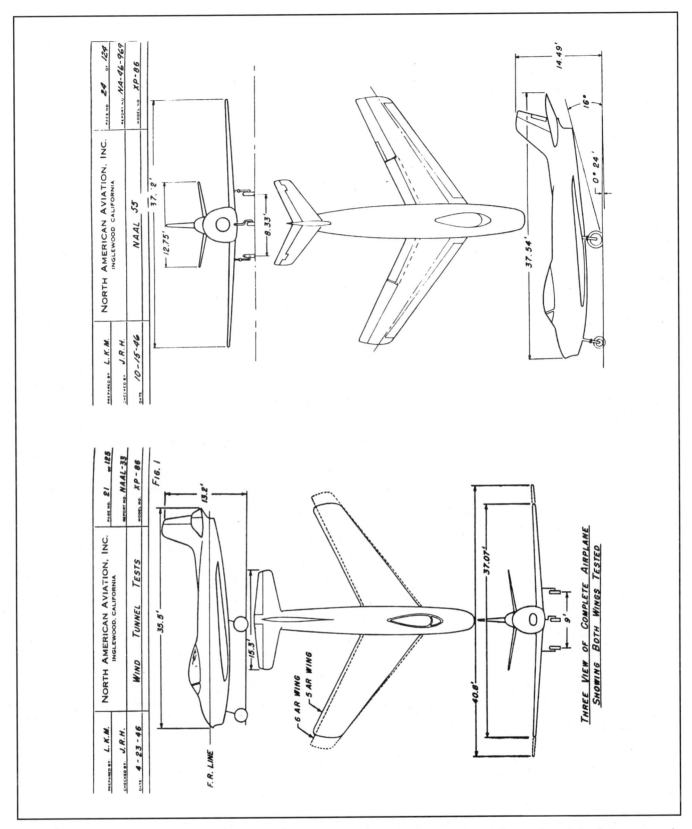

This pair of drawings shows how the XP-86 design evolved. The top drawing shows that in the original concept, only the wings were swept, while the tail assembly remained a straight planform. The overall fuselage was unchanged in going from straight to swept wings. Both 5 and 6 Aspect Ratio wings were tested in the wind tunnel, with the 5AR wing being chosen for production. The later set of drawings show the design with swept wing and tail surfaces, with a circular intake opening replacing the oval shape of the XP-86/XFJ-1 design.

The XP-86 #1 prototype on the ramp at Muroc Dry Lake Airbase (now Edwards Flight Test Center)in December 1947. The XP-86 was rolled out on August 8th 1947, with the first flight taking place on October 1st 1947. Note all the instrument probes under the fuselage, atop the vertical fin, and on both wingtips. The pitot head was inside the intake duct, as it was on production F-86As. Note the single-piece, non-folding nose gear door, which was modified on production airplanes. (USAFM)

The XP-86 differed considerably from its Navy cousin, now designated the XFJ-1. North American refined the fuselage shape and deleted many of the things designed to aid in low speed performance that were required for aircraft carrier landings. The XP-86 wing had the same planform as the XFJ-1, but the airfoil was much thinner. On both the upper and lower wing surfaces were the dive brakes, borrowed directly from the A-36A version of the Mustang. The fuselage had a much higher fineness ratio than the XFJ-1, and the intake was oval in shape. Power was the same for both aircraft—the General Electric TG 180 (J35). The

TG 180 had an eleven stage, axial flow compressor, and offered 4,000 lbs. of thrust.

The XP-86 had a pressurized cockpit, hydraulic elevator and aileron boost, and had wingtip fuel tanks that could be jettisoned in emergencies. Armament was the standard for Army Air Force aircraft—six .50 caliber M3 machine guns in the nose, with 267 rounds per gun. The gunsight was the A-1 type, with a AN/APG-5 radar range finder. Under the wings, a pair of pylons could hold up to 2,000 lbs. of bombs, drop tanks, or eight 5" HVAR rockets.

The XP-86 was 35.5 feet in length, 13.2 feet in height, with a wingspan of 58.2 feet. With a maximum gross weight of 14,600 lbs., the TG 180-powered XP-86 was estimated to have a rate of climb of 5520'/min, a combat range of 1500 miles, a ferry range of 2240 miles when 170 gallon wingtip tanks were installed, and a service ceiling of 44,900'. But the speed was estimated to be only 582 MPH at 10,000'—far below the GOR requirement of 600+ MPH.

On June 20, 1945, the mock-up of the XP-86 was unveiled at the North American plant in Inglewood, California. Very sleek in its gloss Pearl Grey paint, the XP-86

This photo of the #1 prototype with George "Wheaties" Welch at the controls, shows the "PU" buzz number, P for Pursuit, on the lower left wings. Note how the underfuselage dive brake door has been sealed closed with black tape. Close examination of the rear fuselage also shows the rear-opening dive brake doors and actuators. (NAA)

mock-up was quickly approved by Army Air Force officials. Photos of the mock-up show the aft section of the fuselage had its engine break about midway through the wing root chord. The fuselage was much sleeker than the rotund XFJ-1.

But North American officials knew that the lack of speed would eventually kill the XP-86 program

Following the redesign of the dive brake doors, the #1 prototype was re-painted in overall gloss grey, ANA 620, and the (now) correct "FU" buzz number (F for Fighter), has been applied. The production style dive brakes were first slated for testing on the #3 prototype, but were instead, added to the #1 aircraft in January 1948. It was thought that the gloss grey paint would smooth air flow, thus adding speed. But the aircraft was actually slower due to the added weight of the paint. And the paint peeled badly due to fuel leaks and high speed, diminishing the speed even more. (Peter Bowers)

unless something drastic took place, such as a much more powerful gas turbine or some way to reduce the drag encountered at speeds over 500 MPH. It did! For many years, the advantages of sweeping the leading edge of the wing to reduce drag rise had been known. But the disadvantages of the swept wing were many, not the least of which was the loss of stability, especially at low speeds. The Germans had encountered this with the Me-262, which had a slight sweep to the outer wing leading edge. They found that by using a movable leading edge surface, commonly referred to as a "slat," that many of the low speed stability problems could be overcome.

On August 14, 1945, North American Aviation received a research and development grant to develop a swept wing for the XP-86. Two weeks later a .23 scale model of a swept wing XP-86 was built. On September 18, 1945, the XP-86 model was wind tunnel tested. The results were exactly what North American and Army Air Force had been looking for. The swept wing lowered the drag rise and compressibility enough that it brought the XP-86 into the 600+ MPH range, even using available gas turbine technology. On November 1, 1945, Army Air Force approved the "new" swept wing version of the XP-86.

XP-86 Swept Wing Development

The decision to radically re-design the XP-86 was both easy and difficult for North American officials. With the re-design, all costs already incurred on the straight wing NA-140 jet fighter would have to be absorbed by the company. Some of this would be recouped through the decision by the US Navy to go ahead with production of the XFJ-1 Fury. However, it was quite easy for North American to make such a drastic move in as much as the NA-140 would never be able to meet the Army Air Force General Operational Requirement, which included a top speed in excess of 600 MPH. The thin straight wing simply would not allow that type of speed no matter how much power was available.

Sweeping the wing had long been known as one of the answers to lower drag and compressibility problems associated with high performance airplanes operating at or near Mach One. As early as 1942 North American Aviation engineers were working on several swept wing projects, including a *forward* swept wing P-51 design study. But the problems associated with sweeping the wing were as great as the end results. Sweeping the wing

Underwing drop tank designs were tested on all three prototypes. Note how this 200 gallon tank design was "faired in" to the underside of the wing, almost actually touching the wing. Tests, both wind tunnel and flight tests, revealed that the best design for a "combat tank" was a banana shape that was flat on the top matching the underside of the wing. (USAFM)

did lower the thickness ratio, which would result in higher speeds. But sweeping the wing also created wing tip stall and low speed stability problems. Problems that no one had been able to overcome.

On August 24th 1944, Mr. Ed Horkey, a North American design engineer, went to Langley Field to study the effects of using a very thin wing on airplanes operating at higher Mach numbers. Mr. Horkey was informed by Langley officials that no test data existed for such a design, let alone a swept wing. In early 1945 Allied forces overran several German aircraft manufacturing and test facilities, including one that was conducting research into the effects of wing sweep. The Messerschmitt Me-262 jet fighter had a mild (15°) sweep to the leading edge of its wing. It was also discovered that Messerschmitt had been working on a radically swept (35°) version of the Me-262. Luckily, the war ended before German technology could overcome the stability problems of such a drastically swept wing. As more and more captured German data became available, the benefits of wing sweep, i.e., delaying the compressibility drag rise, were clearly confirmed.

It was Mr. Larry Green, head of Design Aerodynamics at North American, that finally came up with an answer to the problems of instability in the swept wing. Green, taking night school courses in technical German, began translating all the material being funneled to North American by Wright Field.

The #3 aircraft was the only prototype carrying full armament, including six .50 caliber machine guns in the nose, and sixteen 5" High Velocity Aircraft Rockets (HVARs) under the wings. Tests were also flown with a pair of 500 lb. bombs. (USAFM)

Within the captured material was considerable data concerning the use of wing leading edge movable surfaces, commonly called SLATS, as a possible solution to the instability problems. The North American Aerodynamics Group, headed by Ed Horkey, finally convinced the pow-ers-that-be that wing sweep would put the XP-86 over the top as far as the speed requirement of the G.O.R. was concerned. In August 1945, "Dutch" Kindelberger, President of North American, approved funding for wind tunnel tests and further design studies on

The type A-1CM gun sight was used on all F-86s from F-86A through F-86F-5, before being changed for the type A-4. It was incorporated with the APG-30 ranging radar. You simply "dialed in" the wingspan of the opposing aircraft (a MiG-15 was 33') and closed until the target indicator light glowed. Then pulled the trigger. Of course, the other guy is "jinking" all over the sky to keep you from doing just that.

the swept wing XP-86 proposal for the Army Air Force. On November 1st 1945, General Bill Craigie, head of Research & Development at Wright Field, gave North American the go ahead for the swept wing XP-86.

The original straight wing XP-86 fuselage and tail assembly was mated to a 35° swept wing, similar to that found on the advanced Me-262 proposal. Wind tunnel tests confirmed the lower drag resulting in higher speeds—and the instabil-ity problems. However, Green convinced the North American engineering staff that these problems could be overcome through the use of a movable leading edge slat. Slowly but surely, the North American engineers brought the design to its final shape. But the slat design remained a problem. Finally, an entire Me-262 wing was flown in from Wright Field. North American's engineers disassembled the slats and modified the slat track mechanism to fit the XP-86 wing. The engineers also used the slat lock and control switch from the Me-262. Although not perfect, it was at least a start and the slat worked.

Both 5 and 6 Aspect wings (the ratio between average span and chord) were tested in the tunnel, before finally settling on a 5 aspect wing having a 35° sweep. Originally, the swept wing proposal retained the straight tail assembly from the XP-86. However, by the time the XP-86 mock-up was being built, both the vertical and horizontal tail surfaces were also swept at 35°.

Mechanics of the 1st Fighter Group work on an early F-86A at March AFB, California in early 1949. Note how the dive brakes hinge at the front, and open at an angle into the air stream. Inside the tail pipe opening can be seen a pair of "rats" or "mice," which were installed to increase the exhaust temperature, thus increasing thrust, thus giving greater speed. Of course, "ratting the tailpipe" excessively could, and did, burn the tail pipe. (NAA)

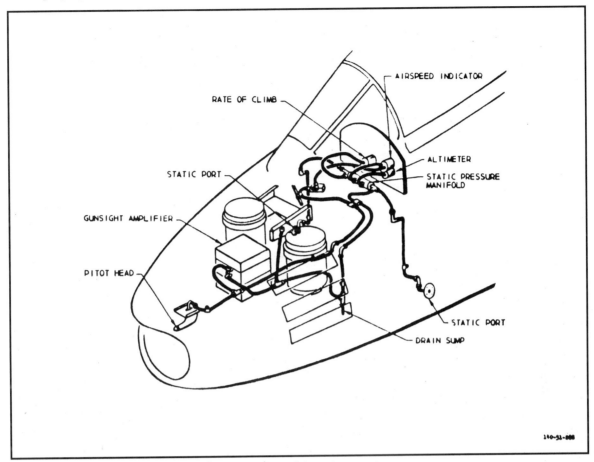

Figure 3-40. Pitot-Static System

are identified by colored tape, the pitot pressure lines being coded black, and the static lines green and black. To facilitate proper connection of the lines, the fittings on the lines and instrument cases are stamped with the letters "S" (static) and "P" (pressure)..

3-217. INSTRUMENTS.

3-218. The following table is a list of all instruments, indicators, and miscellaneous associated equipment installed in the airplane. The table is divided into three sections: flight, engine, and miscellaneous. The last column in the table shows the source of operating supply for all instruments. Refer to figure 3-41 for a schematic diagram of the instrument system.

FLIGHT INSTRUMENTS

INSTRUMENT	TYPE OR NO.	OPERATING SOURCE
Airspeed Indicator	F-4. Spec. No. 94-27512	A
Rate-of-Climb Indicator	AN5825T3	A
Turn-and-Bank Indicator	AN5819T3	B
Altimeter	AN5760T2A	A
Attitude Gyro	J-1, Spec. No. 27561	B
Gyrosyn Compass	Spec. No. 27527	B
Magnetic Stand-by Compass	B-21, Spec. No. 27471A	D
Clock	AN5743T1A	D
**Radio Compass	1D90/ARN-6	F

** Airplanes AAF45-59598 and AAF45-59599

The pitot head on all the prototype and F-86A aircraft was inside the air intake duct, not on the right wingtip as normally seen on F-86s. The pitot head was moved to the right wingtip with the F-86E and retrofitted to F-86A models as they were updated to F-86A-6 and A-7 specifications.

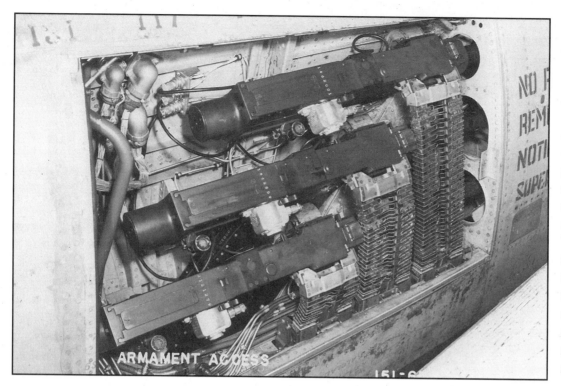

The right bank of M3 .50 caliber machine guns, which was the standard armament of all day fighter variants of the F-86. Each gun was electrically charged, and had a cyclic rate of 1100 rounds per minute. The guns were fed from ammunition bays under the weapons bay, with each ammunition canister holding a maximum of 300 rounds. (NAA)

Additionally, the horizontal stabilizer was fully adjustable to achieve a better balance between low speed control and high speed flight requirements.

Sweeping the tail surfaces, increased overall length two feet. The cockpit sat high on the forward fuselage and had a full, blown PlexiGlas canopy that offered excellent all-round vision (360°) for the pilot. It was something that would not be matched in any fighter aircraft until the McDonnell/Douglas F-15 Eagle was unveiled some 25 years later. The XP-86 was to have three speed brake doors—a pair of smaller doors on the rear fuselage sides that opened to the rear; and a larger slab door under the rear fuselage.

The XP-86 was to be armed with six .50 caliber M3 machine guns mounted in banks of three on either side of the cockpit. Ammunition bays were in the bottom of the fuselage under the gun bay, each "can" holding a maximum of 300 rounds, although 267 rounds was the normal loading. The gun muzzles were recessed behind individual "doors" that opened in 1/20th of a second when the trigger was pulled. All radio and radar antennas were to be enclosed in fiberglass fairings within the design of the aircraft. The engine that would power the prototype was the Chevrolet-built, General Electric J35-C-3 rated at 4,000 lbs. static thrust. However, production aircraft were slated to

Sgt. Melvin Clapp adjusts the ejector seat of a 4th FIG F-86A at Kimpo in the summer of 1951. The F-86A was one of the first Air Force aircraft to employ an ejector seat due to the high speeds the aircraft could attain. The seat worked in conjunction with the canopy extraction system; the pilot first blew off the canopy with one trigger, then pulled the second which ejected the seat. The seat was not armored, and had a wooden back for pilot "comfort." (USAF)

WARBIRDTECH
SERIES

North American production personnel install the control stick in the cockpit of the 393rd F-86A built on the Inglewood assembly line. All interior equipment bays were painted Interior Green, FS 34151. North American built a total of 554 F-86A models at their Inglewood assembly plant. (NAA)

be powered by the GE TG190 (J47) engine offering 5,000 lbs. static thrust.

The design of the wing wasn't the only new innovation found within the XP-86 design. The wing was of a totally new construction and manufacturing process. The conventional "rib and stringer" wing construction was replaced by a double skin structure with "hat sections" between the layers. The wing skins were tapered throughout their length and width, being .250" thick at the wing root, tapering down to .064"at the joint with the outer wing skin, and .032" at the wing tip. So complex were these tapered skins that they required special milling machines. It took over 45 minutes to complete a single skin. The fuselage was unique in that it was divided into two sections, joined near the wing trailing edge. Splitting the fuselage at this juncture provided easy access to the engines and accessories. Easy access to the equipment in the nose area, was supplied through doors having continuous hinges.

On February 28th, 1946, the mock-up of the swept wing XP-86 received Army Air Force approval. And in August 1946, basic engineering drawings were made available to the manu-facturing division of North American, and metal was finally cut for the new airplane. So excited was Army Air Force over the prospect of the new swept wing XP-86, and its projected much higher perfor-

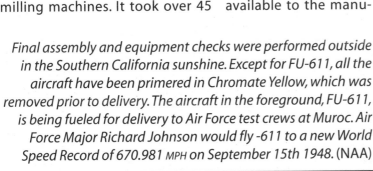

Final assembly and equipment checks were performed outside in the Southern California sunshine. Except for FU-611, all the aircraft have been primered in Chromate Yellow, which was removed prior to delivery. The aircraft in the foreground, FU-611, is being fueled for delivery to Air Force test crews at Muroc. Air Force Major Richard Johnson would fly -611 to a new World Speed Record of 670.981 MPH on September 15th 1948. (NAA)

mance, that a letter contract was awarded to North American on December 20th, 1946, to build 33 production P-86As. No YP-86 service test aircraft were built. On August 8th, 1947, the wait was over. On that morning, the doors of North American's Inglewood factory opened to reveal the first swept wing production aircraft in the world—XP-86 #1, serial 45-59597. Six days later the 689 Board completed its inspection of the first prototype.

During the next month, North American engineers conducted taxi and brake tests at Mines Field, which adjoined the North American factory at Inglewood (Mines Field is now Los Angeles International Airport). On September 11th 1947, the XP-86 was disassembled and trucked to the North base area of Muroc Dry Lake Army Air Base, now known as Edwards AFB. The XP-86 was then re-assembled and all systems retested and adjusted in anticipation of the first flight. On the morning of October 1st 1947, George "Wheaties" Welch, Chief Test Pilot

for North American, taxied the XP-86 to the edge of the runway at Muroc. Welch released the brakes and pushed the throttle on the J35 forward. Three thousand feet down the runway at Muroc, the XP-86 lifted smoothly off the dry lake bed runway for the first time.

Everything about the first flight went smoothly, and 30 minutes later Welch made a final circuit over the base, pulled the lever to lower the landing gear, and began his approach for a landing. Ed Horkey recalls, "Ed Virgin, Head of Engineering Flight Test, Jim Sullivan, and I were clustered around the ground radio listening to George's excited chatter about the first flight. The first flight went very smoothly, with each item on the First Flight Card being checked off satisfactorily. George could tell from the speeds he was obtaining, versus the power settings on the J35, that he was riding something that was pretty fast. After about a 30 minute flight, it became time to land and George lowered the flaps and landing gear."

"The main gear lock lights were in the green, but the nose wheel light did not show the gear was down and locked. We had him make a pass, and we could clearly see the nose gear was down about 45°. George tried everything he and we could think of—but nothing worked. Decision time was rapidly coming upon us. Ed Virgin and I were immediately unanimous in letting George make the decision on whether to jump or bring the airplane in. The company would not influence a decision to save the airplane if it meant jeopardizing George's life."

"George radioed in that he was

A crew chief checks the 5" HVARs mounted in pairs under the wings of a Air Training Command F-86A from the Fighter School at Nellis AFB, Nevada. The F-86A could carry up to sixteen HVARs if no underwing drop tanks were installed. (NAA)

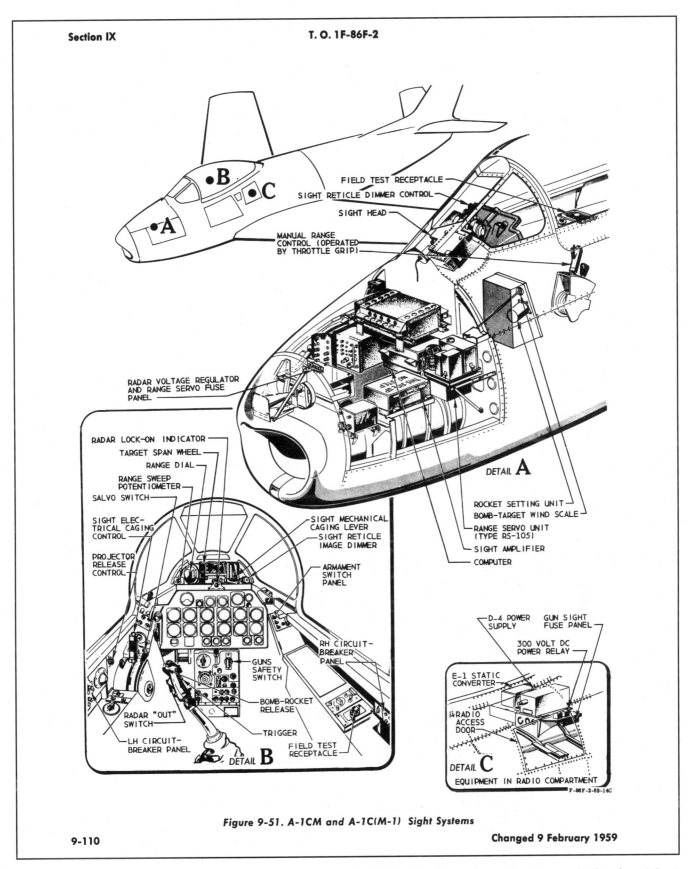

FIELD TEST RECEPTACLE
SIGHT RETICLE DIMMER CONTROL
SIGHT HEAD
MANUAL RANGE CONTROL (OPERATED BY THROTTLE GRIP)

RADAR VOLTAGE REGULATOR AND RANGE SERVO FUSE PANEL

DETAIL A

ROCKET SETTING UNIT
BOMB-TARGET WIND SCALE
RANGE SERVO UNIT (TYPE RS-105)
SIGHT AMPLIFIER
COMPUTER

RADAR LOCK-ON INDICATOR
TARGET SPAN WHEEL
RANGE DIAL
RANGE SWEEP POTENTIOMETER
SALVO SWITCH
SIGHT ELECTRICAL CAGING CONTROL
PROJECTOR RELEASE CONTROL
RADAR "OUT" SWITCH
LH CIRCUIT-BREAKER PANEL

SIGHT MECHANICAL CAGING LEVER
SIGHT RETICLE IMAGE DIMMER
ARMAMENT SWITCH PANEL
RH CIRCUIT-BREAKER PANEL
GUNS SAFETY SWITCH
BOMB-ROCKET RELEASE
TRIGGER
FIELD TEST RECEPTACLE

DETAIL B

D-4 POWER SUPPLY
GUN SIGHT FUSE PANEL
300 VOLT DC POWER RELAY
E-1 STATIC CONVERTER
RADIO ACCESS DOOR

DETAIL C
EQUIPMENT IN RADIO COMPARTMENT

F-86F-2-69-14C

Figure 9-51. A-1CM and A-1C(M-1) Sight Systems

Changed 9 February 1959

This drawing shows all the equipment that makes up the AN/APG-30 radar and type A-1CM gun sight. The APG-30 radar had a range of from 450 to 9000 feet, although air to air victories were rarely attained or attempted outside of 1000' range.

Drop tank development for the F-86 was an ongoing thing with both Air Force and North American. This is one of the first designs of the 120 gallon so-called "combat tanks," which were supposed to increase the range without sacrificing speed or maneuverability. Note the straight across tail fins, which were replaced with ones having a negative dihedral on production tanks. (USAFM)

An F-86A-5 exhibiting all the various weapons that it could carry including 1800 rounds of .50 caliber ammunition, 5" HVARs, 500 lb. and 1000 lb. bombs, packages of cluster bomblets, and chemical tanks. The aircraft has 120 gallon combat tanks installed under the wings. (NAA)

going to stay with the airplane and try to bring her home. But he was going to try the landing on the dry lake bed and not on one of the runways. He made a smooth, very nose high approach. Touching down on the lake bed, George let the airplane just coast along with no brake application. As the airplane slowed and the nose started irretrievably over, the nose gear swung forward and locked into place just as the tire contacted the lake bed. The only thing heard on the radio was George quietly exclaiming over and over, 'Lucky! Lucky!'"

"We found out later that someone in landing gear design or hydraulics was not impressed with the nose gear load data that had been furnished them by the wind tunnel and aerodynamics crew. They installed a cylinder/piston size on the nose gear retraction system that was easy to obtain—not the one called for in the specs. Normally, nose wheels rotated down to the rear, so that air loads would make sure the gear came down even if the hydraulics failed. However, the XP-86 nose intake duct layout precluded this approach, and the nose gear rotated down toward the front, against the air stream! The immediate fix on the XP-86 was to use two of the cylinder/pistons found on the original system, then replace them later with the larger, correct one. No further problems occurred."

Other than the nose gear problem, Welch had only one complaint about that first flight in the XP-86. The J35 didn't produce enough power! With only 4,000 lbs. of static thrust, the XP-86 had a rate of climb of only 4,000 ft./min. But since the J35 was not the engine slated to power the production airplanes, no

one got too excited. Production P-86As would have J47 power with 5,000 lbs. thrust available. Especially in light of what happened next while still using J35 power.

On October 14th 1947, Chuck Yeager took the Bell XS-1 beyond the magic number of Mach 1.0— the first piloted vehicle to do so. But George Welch may have beaten that date in history during some of the routine tests with the XP-86. Welch began complaining to the engineers about some unusual fluctuations in his airspeed and altitude indicators. During flight in the transonic range close to Mach 1.0, shock waves will effect both the airspeed and altimeter readings.

Ed Horkey again recalls; "Had George gone Mach 1 before October 14th 1947? This is an intriguing question. But recently discovered data in the North American archives seem to indicate that possibility. Following the first flight and corrections to the nose gear assembly, the rest of North American's Phase One Flight Tests up to Flight 32, showed a great capability of the airplane to fly, analyze the data, make required changes, and fly again quickly. Following George's complaints about the airspeed and altimeter readings, we started to check into the problem. But at that time, North American had no way of calibrating airspeed indicators into the transonic range."

Compared with its predecessor, the P-51D Mustang, the instrument panel of the F-86A was quite complicated. Added to the normal flight instruments showing speed, altitude, and attitude, are exhaust gas temperature, outside air temperature, and G meters—all necessary with the high speeds the F-86 attained. Note the Slat Lock Control on the upper left side of the instrument shroud. (USAF)

"The NACA had set up a flight test operation at Muroc, later known as Dryden Center. They put a tracking theodolite (like a surveyors transit) together with a large radar receiver and could measure speeds very accurately at any altitude above Muroc. We heard about it and talked Walt Williams, NACA Director, into tracking George in the XP-86. They asked Welch to dive the XP-86 in a certain pattern, after which they would give us his speed and Mach number. Lo and behold! George hit a reading of Mach 1.02 and 1.03. The date was November

F-86A 47-611 was used as an armament test bed in addition to setting the World Speed Record. It was "hung" from a crane when first testing the 5" HVARs at Muroc, before any live-fire flight tests were performed. (USAFM)

21st 1947. But George had been performing some of those very same flight patterns during tests before October 14th 1947!"

"Just like the people involved in the XS-1 program, everyone involved in the XP-86 flight test program was immediately sworn to secrecy. In fact, Stuart Symington, the first Secretary of the independent United States Air Force, called Dutch Kindelberger shortly thereafter, and told him not to let anything out concerning the XP-86 going over Mach 0.94. It would be a secret for almost 50 years!"

Even if George Welch did not exceed Mach 1.0 during those early Phase I tests (tests flown by North American company pilots), the Air Force was duly impressed. On October 16th 1947, Fixed Price Contract W33-038-ac-16013 was granted to North American Aviation, authorizing production of 33 P-86A aircraft. This contract was supplemented on that same day to include production of 190 P-86B aircraft. The P-86B was a strengthened P-86A, with beefier landing gear for rough field operations, and an upgraded J47 engine. The P-86B fuselage would have been widened 7 inches to make room in the fuselage for the larger wheels and tires. But advancements in both tires and brake systems nullified the need for the P-86B, and the contract was amended on December 1st 1947, changing the production order to an additional 188 P-86As and 2 P-86Cs.

Phase II Flight tests (tests flown by Air Force pilots) began in early December 1947. Major Ken Chilstrom was the Phase 2 Air Force pilot. "In late November 1947, North American Aviation called Colonel Al Boyd, Chief of Air Force Flight Test Division, and recommended delaying the start of the Phase II flight tests because of heavy rains at Muroc, resulting in flooding of the dry lake bed. Colonel Boyd suggest-

The first group to receive the F-86A was the 1st Fighter Group at March AFB, California, with their first F-86A-1s arriving in February 1949. This photo of the March AFB ramp shows eighteen F-86A-5s in the summer of 1949. The A-5 had the V-shaped armored windscreen. The light grey areas on the fuselage, fin, and wingtips are natural fiberglass areas covering various antennas. Note the 206.5 gallon underwing "ferry tanks." (Peter Bowers)

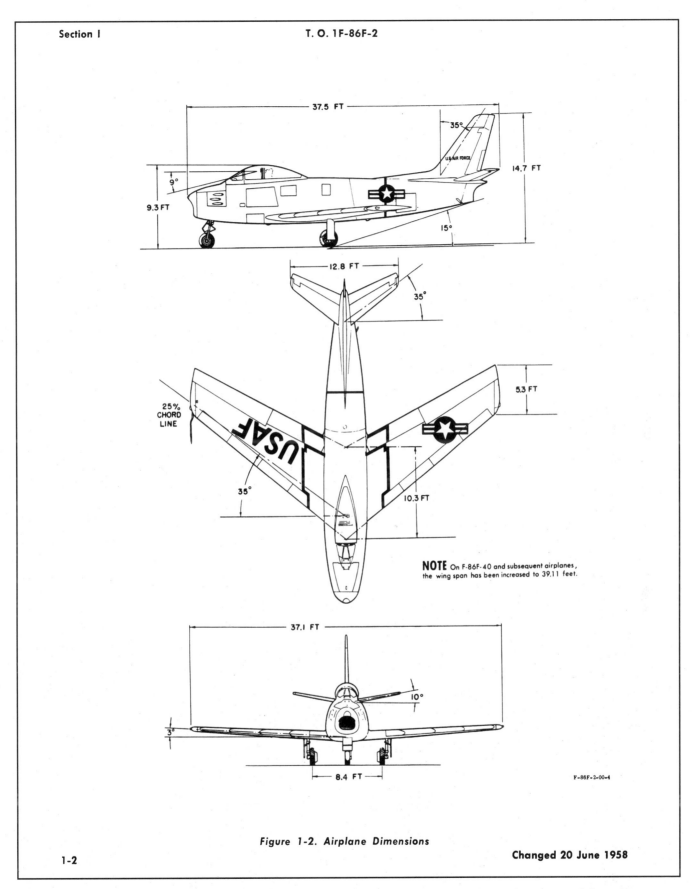

NOTE On F-86F-40 and subsequent airplanes, the wing span has been increased to 39.11 feet.

F-86F-2-00-4

Figure 1-2. Airplane Dimensions

Airplane dimensions for the F-86 remained essentially the same from XP-86 through all variants of the F-86F, except for the angle of the wing leading edge which increased to 37° when the "6-3 leading edge wing" was installed.

An F-86A-1 from the 71st FIS in the 1st FIG during mid-1950. In April 1950, the 1st FG was transferred to Air Defense Command and re-designated as a Fighter Interceptor Group. The aircraft were painted with a flash of color representing each squadron, Red for the 71st FIS, on the fuselage sides, along with the 1st FIG badge and a squadron emblem. (Bob Esposito)

ed I visit Muroc and inspect the conditions to determine if I could operate from the runway at North Base. After a few days at North Base evaluating the lake bed, the runway, and the XP-86, I called Colonel Boyd and recommended we proceed with Phase II tests using North Base."

"Colonel Boyd notified North American that the Air Force would begin flying the Phase II tests of the XP-86 immediately. North American expressed concern because of the extremely short runway conditions at North Base. However, the Air Force prevailed and I made my first take off on December 2nd 1947. This flight was a get acquainted flight, and since there were no squawks, I asked that the XP-86 be refueled for a second flight that day! This allowed for performance checks and speed points at intermediate altitudes."

"I was very impressed with the XP-86's speed improvement over the Republic P-84 Thunderjet with the same engine, but having a straight wing. The maximum speed for the XP-84 was 615 MPH, while the XP-86 maximum speed was in excess of 650 MPH! Our remaining Phase II flights were accomplished in 11 flights totaling 10 hours and 17 minutes—all in six days! The XP-86s performance envelope was investigated up to Mach 0.9, and altitudes near 45,000 feet. Unfortunately, the cabin pressurization system was inoperative, and the heating system at 45,000 feet was uncomfortable. I did not realize until later that the XP-86's oxygen system lacked a safety margin for flying in an unpressurized cabin! My conclusion to the Phase II tests, and supported by our data, was that the Air Force now had the very best jet fighter developed to this date, anywhere in the world."

In early 1948, XP-86 prototypes #2 (45-59598) and #3 (45-59599) became available for testing. They were different from the #1 airplane, as well as different from each other in several areas. Both #1 and #2 had different fuel gauges, a stall warning system built into the control stick, a by-pass for emergency operation of the hydraulic boost

Capt. Richard Creighton set a new World Speed Record when he flew this 71st FIS F-86A from San Francisco to Los Angeles on May 20th 1950. Capt. Creighton would later go to Korea and serve with the veteran 4th FIG, shooting down five MiG-15s. (Brig. Gen. Robin Olds)

WARBIRD**TECH**
S E R I E S

system, and hydraulically actuated leading edge slat locks. The #1 bird was the only one to have an on-board fire extinguisher. The #3 prototype was the only XP-86 with fully automatic leading edge slats that opened at 135 MPH, and the only prototype with full armament, including a type Mk.18 gyroscopic gun sight with manual ranging. Both #2 and #3 were equipped with SCR-695-B Identification Friend or Foe beacons, and the AN/ARN-6 radio compass set. Finally, the #1 airplane was the only one with the reverse, or rear-opening side fuselage dive brakes, in addition to having the large ventral brake door under the fuselage.

The spring of 1948 saw many significant events take place in the early P-86 development program. In March, the first P-86A production airplane, 47-605, come off the assembly line at Inglewood. The 689 Board passed it on March 15th. In May the rest of the world was informed that George Welch had exceeded Mach 1.0 in the XP-86, the first airplane to do so (airplane being defined as a vehicle that takes off from the ground, flies, then returns and lands—all under its own power). But the date was set at April 26th 1948!

This flight did take place, but George Welch wasn't the pilot. Ed Horkey recalls the day; "A visiting British pilot came over and was checked out in the XP-86. He was told about the phenomenon he might encounter (i.e., breaking the sonic barrier), and the secrecy restrictions. Unfortunately, he had an open radio channel and all the nearby towers got an earful of his going through Mach 1.0. I understand that he was severely disciplined. However, the facts soon

A pair of 33rd FIG F-86As demonstrate a novel emergency start procedure that was used with some success during the early 1950s. One Sabre was backed up near the "dead" F-86, and directed his jet exhaust into the open air intake of the aircraft behind. This would cause the turbine blades of the "dead" aircraft to start spinning. If the pilot was lucky, he would hit the starter switch and bingo. Tried in Korea, the method was very hard on the fiberglass nose of the F-86A. (USAF)

The third unit to convert to F-86As was the 81st FG based at Kirtland AFB, New Mexico. The 81st was re-designated a Fighter Interceptor Group in January 1950. These 93rd FIS F-86As wait in the Kirtland AFB "alert barns" for the klaxon to sound a scramble, as part of the Albuquerque Air Defense Sector protecting the atom bomb plant at Los Alamos. (Larry Davis)

became common knowledge throughout the aviation industry. I suppose the media never brought it to the public's attention, which would tarnish the otherwise exotic story they already had (Yeager and the XS-1). The June 14th 1948 issue of Aviation Week announced to the world that the XP-86 had gone supersonic."

It has been said that the April 26th flight took place after the XP-86 had been re-engined with the General Electric TG-190 (J47) engine rated at 5,000 lbs. static thrust. But that didn't take place until later in the XP-86 test program. On May 20th, the first flight of a production P-86A took place. Air Force accepted its first two P-86As on May 28th. The very next day, Air Force officials placed a verbal order for an additional 333 P-86As, bringing the total production of the P-86A/F-86A to 554 airplanes. On September 16th 1947, the United States Congress made the Air Force a separate branch of service from its original parent, the US Army. And in June 1948, the new US Air Force re-designated all Pursuit aircraft to Fighter aircraft, changing the prefix from P to F. Thus all XP and P-86A aircraft became XF and F-86A. The three prototypes continued to serve in various test and evaluation missions well into the 1950s. The #1 airplane crashed and was destroyed in September 1952, while #2 and #3 were retired from service in April 1953.

F-86A—Production Begins

The P-86A-1 (NA-151) was the production version based on the third prototype XP-86—with one big difference. The P-86As would be powered by General Electric J47-GE-1 engines rated at 4850 lbs. of thrust. With J47 power, the performance envelope for the P-86 was greatly increased. With the same gross weight as the XP-86, the P-86A-1 had a top speed in excess of 679 MPH at sea level. The service ceiling was increased over 5,000 ft. to 46,000 ft. And the rate of climb almost doubled, jumping from 4100 ft./min. in the J35 powered XP-86, to 7800 ft./min. in the P-86A-1.

Equipment was the same as

Four F-86As of the 56th FIG leave the runway at Selfridge AFB, Michigan during a practice "scramble" in 1950. The J-47 engine was not very efficient and left dark black smoke trails from unburned fuel wherever they flew. It was one way a Sabre pilot could identify another aircraft at a quick glance—if it smoked, it was friendly! (USAF)

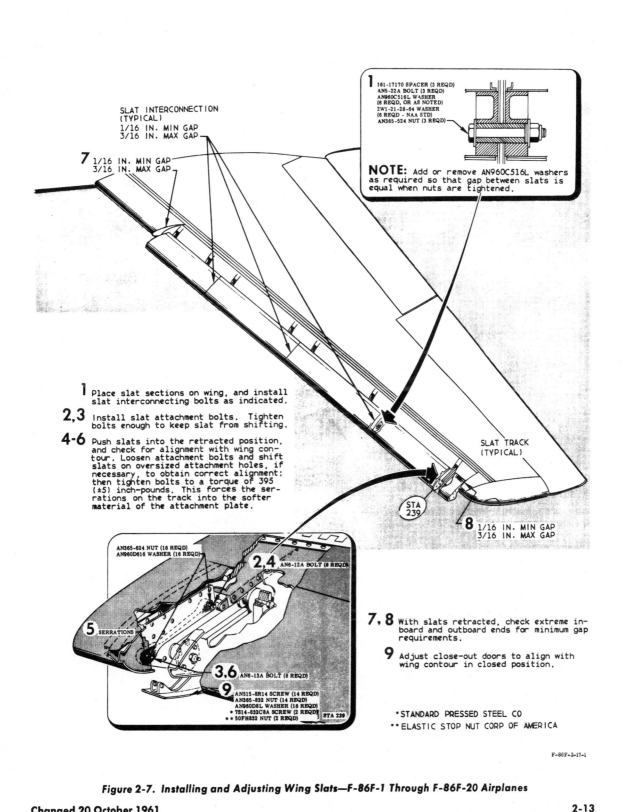

1   161-17170 SPACER (3 REQD)
    AN5-22A BOLT (3 REQD)
    AN960C516L WASHER
    (6 REQD, OR AS NOTED)
    2W1-21-28-64 WASHER
    (6 REQD - NAA STD)
    AN365-524 NUT (3 REQD)

NOTE: Add or remove AN960C516L washers as required so that gap between slats is equal when nuts are tightened.

SLAT INTERCONNECTION (TYPICAL)
1/16 IN. MIN GAP
3/16 IN. MAX GAP

7   1/16 IN. MIN GAP
    3/16 IN. MAX GAP

SLAT TRACK (TYPICAL)

STA 239

8   1/16 IN. MIN GAP
    3/16 IN. MAX GAP

1   Place slat sections on wing, and install slat interconnecting bolts as indicated.

2,3   Install slat attachment bolts. Tighten bolts enough to keep slat from shifting.

4-6   Push slats into the retracted position, and check for alignment with wing contour. Loosen attachment bolts and shift slats on oversized attachment holes, if necessary, to obtain correct alignment; then tighten bolts to a torque of 395 (±5) inch-pounds. This forces the serrations on the track into the softer material of the attachment plate.

AN365-624 NUT (16 REQD)
AN960D616 WASHER (16 REQD)

2,4   AN6-12A BOLT (8 REQD)

5   SERRATIONS

3,6   AN6-13A BOLT (8 REQD)

9   AN515-8R14 SCREW (14 REQD)
    AN365-832 NUT (14 REQD)
    AN960D8L WASHER (16 REQD)
    * 7S14-832C8A SCREW (2 REQD)
    ** 50FH832 NUT (2 REQD)   STA 239

7, 8   With slats retracted, check extreme inboard and outboard ends for minimum gap requirements.

9   Adjust close-out doors to align with wing contour in closed position.

* STANDARD PRESSED STEEL CO

** ELASTIC STOP NUT CORP OF AMERICA

F-86F-2-17-1

Figure 2-7. Installing and Adjusting Wing Slats—F-86F-1 Through F-86F-20 Airplanes

This drawing shows the leading edge slats and actuating devices. Note that the slats themselves are three piece, and that seven tracks are used for each slat.

An 81st FIG F-86A-5 gets checked over by North American personnel at Long Beach prior to the 81st FIG flight to Great Britain in August 1951. The 81st FIG was the first unit to be stationed in Great Britain since the end of World War Two, with its three squadrons being based at RAF Shepards Grove. (David Menard)

found on the third prototype. The P-86A-1s carried six .50 caliber M3 machine guns, with 300 round magazines. The P-86A-1 could carry a pair of 206.5 gallon underwing dropable "ferry tanks." or a pair of 1000 lb. bombs, or sixteen 5 inch rockets on removable, zero length launch stubs. The gun sight was the proven type Mk 18 gyroscopic gun sight with manual ranging. Communications and IFF equipment was the same as on the XP-86. Although all the XP-86s and P-86A-1s were equipped with the

The last group to convert to F-86As was the 23rd FIG based at Presque Isle AFB, Maine in January 1951. This photo was taken in the Fall of 1953 as the "US AIR FORCE" logo did not begin to appear on aircraft until the summer of 1953. These F-86As have all been updated to A-7 specifications, which included wingtip mounted pitot, gun blast door deletion, and AN/APG-30 radar. (Larry Davis)

An early F-86A-5 assigned to the 56th FIG at Selfridge in 1951. The aircraft was originally assigned to the 4th FIG. But when the 4th went to Korea in November 1950, they "swapped" some of their older F-86As for newer models taken from other units like the 56th. This aircraft has been updated by deleting the gun blast "doors" that were standard on the early F-86A-5s. (Bob Esposito)

type T-4E-1 ejection seat catapult, the canopy had to be manually jettisoned before ejection. Beginning with the 34th P-86A built, an explosive device jettisoned the canopy prior to seat firing. Finally, in June 1948, Air Force redesignated all Pursuit aircraft to Fighter aircraft, changing the designation from "P" to "F."

There were basically three distinct blocks of F-86As. the first thirty three P-86A-1 aircraft (47-605/-637) that were ordered on the original contract; a second batch of 188 P-86As that were originally ordered as P-86Bs, but re-designated F-86A-5 (48-129/-316); and a final contract (W33-038-ac-21671) authorizing production of an additional 333 F-86A-5s (49-1007/-1339). There were many changes during the production run of the F-86A including; the curved windscreen was replaced

with an armored V-shaped windscreen beginning with the 1st F-86A-5; gun and ammunition bay heaters, stainless steel oil tanks and oil lines were also added beginning with the 34th airplane. A more effective canopy seal and defroster, plus an improved nose gear steering and activation cylinders were added beginning with the 100th airplane built. The slat and slat track mechanism was re-designed and installed beginning with the 160th F-86A built. F-86A-5 production changes also included re-wiring the cockpit and adding a better master brake system.

Also, beginning with the 189th A-5, a completely new underwing drop tank was introduced. These were the so-called 120 gallon "combat tanks." The development of the "combat tank" is a story unto itself. The original drop tanks were 206.5

gallon "ferry tanks." The "ferry tanks" gave the required range extension (1170 miles), but created a high Mach buffet starting around Mach 0.8. Jet combat, usually occurring at Mach 0.9 and above, would require the F-86 pilot to jettison his tanks to reach combat speeds, thus shortening his range and "loiter time" in the combat area. What was needed was a drop tank design that could be retained during combat or flights into the transonic speed ranges, but would not hinder airplane performance at those speeds.

North American engineers set out to solve the problem in 1948. The "ferry tanks" were large, circular vessels, with horizontal winglets at the rear. Wind tunnel tests indicated that the air flow between the wing bottom and the top of the round "ferry tank" was forming strong shock waves between the tank and the wing, creating a severe buffet at speeds in excess of Mach 0.8. Initially, thoughts were given to fairing in the surfaces of the tanks, thus making them more aerodynamic. A pair of tanks were built and installed, but the buffet remained. The "combat tank" would have a flattened top matching the underside of the wing, thus easing the air flow between the tank and wing. Hung on a pylon about 12 inches below the wing, the flat topped tank performed better than the circular tank, but there was still severe buffeting as the aircraft speed increased to near Mach 1.0.

During tests of various underwing ordnance that could be carried by the P-86, it was discovered that certain flat-topped ordnance, in spite of their total lack of streamlining, could be flown at near sonic speeds—with no buffet! The difference was the close proximity of the ordnance to the wing bottom. A new tank pylon was designed that had only six inches clearance between the wing and the top of the tank. This solved the buffet problem, but created a clearance problem between the rear of the tank and the flaps. The rear of the tank was then shortened and swept downward to clear the flaps, with a pair of small fins on the rear. Finally the tank pylon was increased 2 inches in height for maintenance reasons. An external sway brace on the outside of each tank, was added for stability.

During tank jettison tests, it was revealed that the "combat tanks" had a tendency to rotate up at the rear, damaging the bottom of the wing and flap. This was cured by replacing the small horizontal tail fins with fins almost twice as big, and angled down at 17°. The new "combat tank" held only 120 gallons of fuel as opposed to 206.5 gallons in the "ferry tanks." But the range difference between the two tank designs was almost nil due to the aerodynamically superior design of the "combat tank." Ironically, after all the design, testing, and re-design, the F-86 combat pilots in Korea still dropped their tanks as soon as they sighted the MiGs. However, using the combat tanks did allow them to enter the combat arena over the Yalu River at Mach 0.95—something they couldn't have done using the original "ferry tanks."

On May 20th 1948, the first production F-86A-1 (#47-605) took to the air for the first time. The initial batch of 33 A-1s were used in various flight test programs, as well as

Cindee Lind—6th, *an F-86A-7 assigned to the 142nd FIS/Delaware ANG sits on the ramp at Detroit Airport for the July 4th 1955 air show. The pristine condition and large letter "A" indicate the airplane was part of the all-ANG RICKS air race from California to Detroit. Note the gun blast panel is completely taped over.* (David Menard)

WARBIRD**TECH**
SERIES

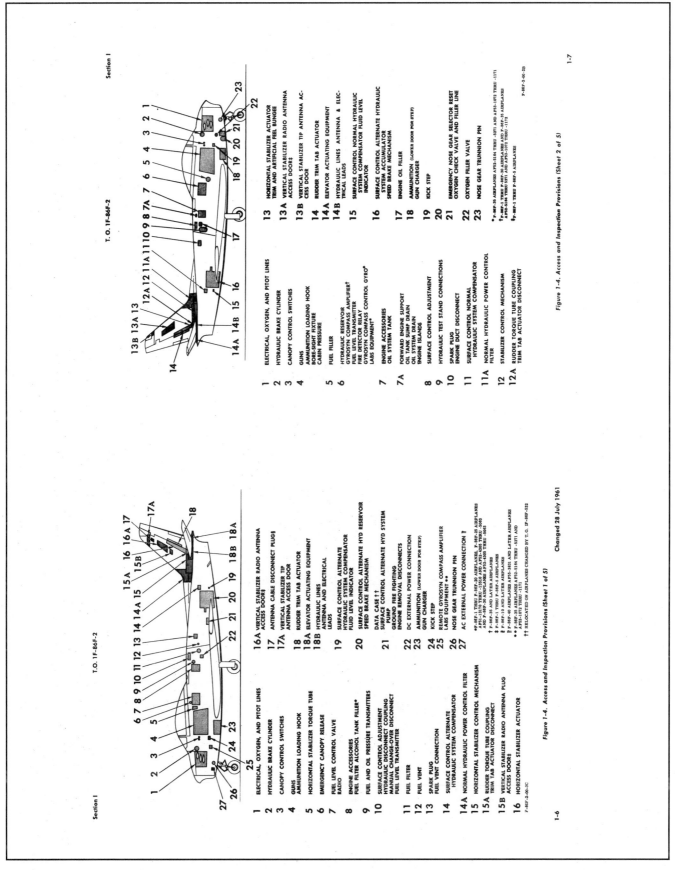

A set of drawings (two above, two on page 33) showing every access door on the typical F-86F, and what each door revealed. With the exception of the vertical tail, these panels were basically the same from F-86A through F-86F.

being the first training F-86s that the Air Force had. Test programs are usually flown by "YF" service test aircraft. But there were no YF-86 service test aircraft authorized under any of the Air Force contracts. The three XP-86s were re-designated YF-86 after being re-engined with the J47 engine. However they were never "officially" re-designated on Air Force record cards. Close examination of the data block found on later photos of the prototypes, however, clearly show it to read "YF-86."

The first two A-1s were delivered to the Air Force on May 28 1948, but both aircraft remained at North American Aviation's Inglewood fac-tory on "bailment" (i.e., on loan) for further testing. Individual A-1 air-craft were assigned different specif-ic missions including; 47-608 being the cold weather test aircraft, -610 flew performance and stability tests at Muroc, -611 was an arma-ment and ordnance test bed, -619 performed structural integrity tests, -609 was bailed to the National Advisory Committee on Aeronautics (NACA). Others per-formed engine control tests, or "paced" other F-86 test flights as no other aircraft type could keep up with an '86! Many were sent to combat units that were slated for conversion training to the F-86.

Two A-1 aircraft played a special role in the early history of the F-86, #47-608 and -611. Besides their pre-viously mentioned missions, these two aircraft were slated to attempt to break the world speed record, which was then being held by a NAVY Douglas D-558-1 SkyStreak at 650.796 MPH. The Air Force ordered a public demonstration of what their new fighter could do, and an attempt on the record at the same time. The site chosen was the Cleveland National Air Race, where General Electric would set up a spe-cial 3 kilometer course over Cleveland Municipal Airport.

Major Richard L. Johnson, a pilot with the Flight Test Section at Wright-Patterson Field, would fly

Sump'N Fishy *and other F-86A-7s from the 115th FIS and 195th FIS, both California ANG squadrons, on the ramp at Van Nuys ANG Base in 1955. The California ANG converted to F-86As in early 1955. The near aircraft,* Sump'N Fishy, *is now on display at the Smithsonian Air and Space Museum. (Joe Bruch)*

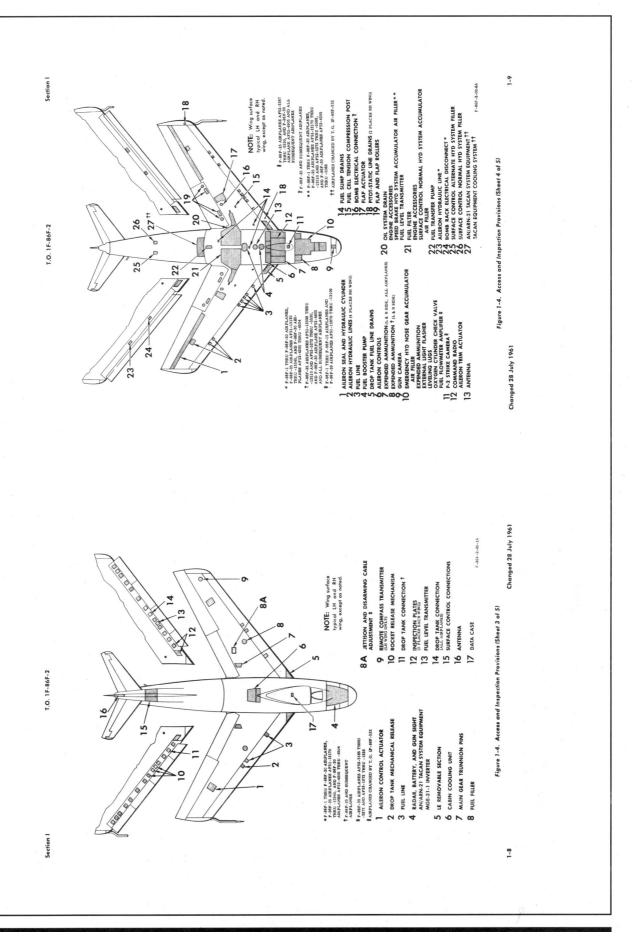

T.O. 1F-86F-2

NOTE: Wing surface typical LH and RH wing, except as noted.

1 AILERON SEAL AND HYDRAULIC CYLINDER
2 AILERON HYDRAULIC LINES (4 PLACES RH WING)
3 FUEL LINE
4 FUEL BOOSTER PUMP
5 DROP TANK FUEL LINE DRAINS
6 AILERON CONTROLS
7 EXPENDED AMMUNITION (L & R SIDE, ALL AIRPLANES)
8 EXPENDED AMMUNITION † (L & R SIDE)
9 GUN CAMERA
10 EMERGENCY HYD NOSE GEAR ACCUMULATOR
   AIR FILLER
   EXPENDED AMMUNITION
   LEVELING LUGS
   OXYGEN CYLINDER CHECK VALVE
   FUEL FLOWMETER AMPLIFIER ‡
11 F-2 STRIKE CAMERA †
12 COMMAND RADIO
   AILERON TRIM ACTUATOR
13 ANTENNA

14 FUEL SUMP DRAINS
15 FUEL CELL TENSION COMPRESSION POST
16 BOMB ELECTRICAL CONNECTION POST
17 FLAP ACTUATOR
18 PITOT-STATIC LINE DRAINS (2 PLACES RH WING)
19 FLAP AND FLAP ROLLERS
20 OIL SYSTEM DRAIN
   ENGINE ACCESSORIES
   SPEED BRAKE HYD SYSTEM ACCUMULATOR AIR FILLER **
   FUEL LEVEL TRANSMITTER
21 FUEL FILTER
   ENGINE ACCESSORIES
   SURFACE CONTROL NORMAL HYD SYSTEM ACCUMULATOR
   AIR FILLER
22 FUEL TRANSFER PUMP
23 AILERON HYDRAULIC LINE *
24 BOMB RACK ELECTRICAL DISCONNECT *
25 SURFACE CONTROL ALTERNATE HYD SYSTEM FILLER
26 SURFACE CONTROL NORMAL HYD SYSTEM FILLER
27 AN/ARN-21 TACAN SYSTEM EQUIPMENT ††
   TACAN EQUIPMENT COOLING SYSTEM ††

* F-86F-1 THRU F-86F-20 AIRPLANES, F-86F-25 AIRPLANES AF52-5387 THRU -5530, AND F-86F-30 AIRPLANE AF52-4505 AND ALL SUBSEQUENT AIRPLANES

** F-86F-25 AND SUBSEQUENT AIRPLANES

† F-86F-25 AIRPLANES AF51-13170 THRU -13510 AND AF52-4805 THRU -5386, AND F-86F-30 AIRPLANES AF53-4305

‡ F-86F-1 THRU F-86F-20 AIRPLANES, F-86F-25 AIRPLANES AF51-13170 THRU -13510 AND AF52-4805 THRU -5386 AND F-86F-20 AIRPLANES AF52-4305 THRU -4604

†† AIRPLANES CHANGED BY T.O. 1F-86F-532

F-86F-2-00-8A

Figure 1-4. Access and Inspection Provisions (Sheet 4 of 5)

Changed 28 July 1961   1-9

T.O. 1F-86F-2

NOTE: Wing surface typical LH and RH wing, except as noted.

8A JETTISON AND DISARMING CABLE
   ADJUSTMENT ‡
9 REMOTE COMPASS TRANSMITTER
   (LH WING ONLY)
10 ROCKET RELEASE MECHANISM
11 DROP TANK CONNECTION †
12 INSPECTION PLATES
   (3 PLACES EACH WING)
13 FUEL LEVEL TRANSMITTER
14 DROP TANK CONNECTION
   (ALL AIRPLANES)
15 SURFACE CONTROL CONNECTIONS
16 ANTENNA
17 DATA CASE

* F-86F-1 THRU F-86F-20 AIRPLANES, F-86F-25 AIRPLANES AF51-13170 THRU -13340, AND F-86F-30 AIRPLANE AF52-4505 THRU -4604

‡ F-86F-25 AIRPLANES AF52-5105 THRU -5271 AND AF53-1078 THRU -1228

8 AIRPLANES CHANGED BY T.O. 1F-86F-532

1 AILERON CONTROL ACTUATOR
2 DROP TANK MECHANICAL RELEASE
3 FUEL LINE
4 RADAR, BATTERY, AND GUN SIGHT
   AN/ARN-21 TACAN SYSTEM EQUIPMENT
   MG-31-1 INVERTER
5 LE REMOVABLE SECTION
6 CABIN COOLING UNIT
7 MAIN GEAR TRUNNION PINS
8 FUEL FILLER

F-86F-2-00-1A

Figure 1-4. Access and Inspection Provisions (Sheet 3 of 5)

Changed 28 July 1961

1-8

A pair of 336th FIS F-86As from Detachment A, leave the runway at Kimpo (K-14) in December 1950. The first seven flyable F-86As went to K-14 on December 13th, and flew their first combat mission on the 17th. Lt. Col. Bruce Hinton scored the first kill by a Sabre over a MiG-15 on that first mission. (Lt. Col. Bruce Hinton)

F-86A-1 47-608, the cold weather test aircraft, for the speed trials held over Labor Day weekend 1948, September 4th, 5th, & 6th. The Federation Aeronautique Internationale (FAI) rules were simple—the airplane could not exceed 500 meters (1640 feet) in height at any time; and during the speed run itself, Major Johnson had to stay below 100 meters (328 ft). This ruled out diving to increase the speed.

An F-86A from the 4th FIG wears camouflage netting on the ramp at Suwon (K-13) in the Summer of 1951. The netting didn't hide the silver F-86s with their black and white wing and fuselage stripes, and was ordered removed by Col. Harrison Thyng. (Bob Makinney)

WARBIRD**TECH**
S E R I E S

A trio of 195th FIS F-86A-7s fly over Los Angeles in 1956. The 195th FIS was based at Van Nuys ANG Base with the 115th FIS. Note that the upper right wing logo reads "ANG" and the last three digits of the serial. This was repeated on the lower left wing. Before the F-86As were put into ANG service, they were sent through the NAA Fresno modification center and brought up to F-86A-6 or A-7 specifications. (Joe Bruch)

Major Johnson took -608 through the course the required six times on Sunday morning, September 5th. Although he averaged 669.480 MPH, the recording cameras caught only three of the passes, thus nullifying the record. Major Johnson was going to try again the next morning but the Ohio weather wouldn't cooperate.

The Air Force then had a similar course laid out over Muroc Dry Lake, which coincidently was the site of most of the F-86 flight test programs. Major Johnson went to Muroc a couple of days following the Cleveland show, where he had the armament test aircraft, 47-611, readied for another attempt at the record. The aircraft was not modified in any way. It was exactly as it had come off the Inglewood

assembly line, with full armament and other combat equipment. On September 15th 1948, the calm air over the high desert of California was just right and Major Johnson made the required six runs successfully. This time the cameras worked on every pass. At altitudes ranging from 75 to 125 feet, Major Johnson was very consistent on each run, with his slowest speed timed at 669.830, and the fastest being 672.762 MPH. When the day was over Major Johnson and the F-86A held a new FAI World Speed Record at 670.781 MPH. The record would stand for over 4 years, until it was broken by another F-86!

Problems with the J47-GE-1 engine that powered the F-86A-1s brought production of the follow-on type, the A-5, to a halt in the

early Fall of 1948. General Electric did supply a few J47-GE-3 engines to North American to get production rolling again. But it wasn't until December 1948, when the J47-GE-7 engine rated at 5340 lbs. of thrust became available, that full production of the A-5 resumed. It was the A-5 that would equip the combat squadrons in the US Air Force. The 94th Fighter Squadron in the 1st Fighter Group, became the first combat squadron to receive the F-86A when two aircraft were delivered to March Field on February 15 1949. By the end of May 1949, the 1st FG was completely equipped (83 aircraft) with F-86A-5s. Coincidently, the 1st FG was charged with the air defense of the Los Angeles area, site of the North American plant.

Col. Glenn Eagleston, a World War Two ace with the 354th FG, ran into a good MiG pilot in June 1951. The MiG pilot shot Eagleston's Sabre to pieces before being driven off by Lt. Col. Bruce Hinton. Several MiG cannon shells struck the gun bay in "Eagle's" Sabre, completely destroying the upper guns—but saving Eagleston's life. The Sabre came 200 miles home to Suwon, where Eagleston made a belly landing.

The next units to convert to F-86s, were the 4th FG near Washington, D.C., and the 81st FG defending the atom bomb facilities in New Mexico. Three other units flew the F-86A in first line USAF service—the 33rd FIG at Otis AFB, the 56th FG at Selfridge AFB, Michigan, and the 23rd FIG at Presque Isle AFB, Maine. During March 1949, the 1st FG held a contest at March Field to put a catchy name on their new aircraft. Unofficially, North American referred to the F-86 as the SILVER CHARGER. But the men of the 1st FG came up with the name SABRE, and the Air Force adopted it officially. Of course, the press quickly modified the name to SABREJET, likening it to other new jet types like the Republic Thunderjet and the Grumman Pantherjet.

Although testing of the F-86A would continue well into the 1950s, the greatest test of all would come far from sunny California during the winter of 1950. On November 1st 1950, the United Nation air forces, especially the US 5th AF, were rudely introduced to the Sabre's contemporary in the skies over North Korea—the Mikoyan-Gurevich type 15 or MiG-15. The 4th FIG, led by such World War 2 veterans as Vermont Garrison, John Meyer, and Glenn Eagleston, were alerted for duty in Korea one short week after the MiGs appeared. It was the most successful test of all, with almost 800 MiGs being shot down by 5th AF Sabres—a 10-1 kill ratio!

The lack of drop tanks persisted throughout the combat in Korea. This 4th FIG F-86A was flown to the Far East Air Material Command at Tachikawa AB, Japan, to fly tests for installation of Beech 165 gallon drop tanks, which were based on the Misawa-converted F-80 wingtip tanks. (USAFM)

Throughout the production run and service life of the F-86A-5, many modifications were performed to attempt to make the airplane more reliable or give it better performance. The last 24 A-5s were equipped with the type A-1CM gun sight, replacing the older Mk-18 sight, but still with manual ranging. As airplanes returned from Korea, they were rotated through the North American facility in Fresno, California prior to returning to service with the Air Force or Air National Guard. All the A-5s were brought up to the latest specifications including use of the AN/APG-5C ranging radar working in conjunction with the A-1CM sight. These aircraft were designated F-86A-6. Some were further upgraded with the AN/APG-30 ranging radar and designated A-7. Many were re-engined with the J47-GE-13 engine rated at 5450 lbs. thrust.

As these aircraft left the Fresno modification center, many were slated for service with the first Air National Guard squadrons to equip with the Sabre, the 123rd FIS/Oregon ANG, or the 126th FIS/Wisconsin ANG. However, neither squadron converted to Sabres at the time and the updated A-6s and A-7s went to the remaining F-86A-equipped Air Force squadrons in the 1st, 23rd, 56th, and 81st FIGs. The first F-86As did not enter service with the Air National Guard until the 186th FIS/Montana ANG converted in November 1953. The last F-86As were retired from service in 1960 when the California and Colorado ANGs converted to other types. Except for the single F-86A-5, 49-1069, which was modified to accept the Avro Orenda engine as the prototype for the Canadair Sabre series, no F-86A aircraft were exported to other nations.

ASHTRAY

One minor development that was based on the F-86A was the conversion of several aircraft to photo reconnaissance RF-86As. The entire project was done in the Korean Theater during the war, but then carried on at the production facilities in Los Angeles as part of the F-86F development program. During the early part of the war, photo reconnaissance missions along the Yalu River were flown by RF-51D and RF-80 aircraft with relative impunity. But the introduction of the MiG-15 made the photo recce mission highly dangerous, since the MiG was so much faster than either the RF-51 or the RF-80. What was needed was a photo recon version of the Sabre. But North American had nothing in the planning stages regarding such an aircraft.

Majors Bruce Fish and Ruffin Gray,

De Ramblin Rebel *and* Punkin Head *sit at the end of the ramp at K-13 as mechanics and crew chiefs strip them for useable parts in the Spring of 1951. After they were stripped, they would be moved to the end of the runway, propped up on barrels, and used as decoys during the nightly visits of "Bedcheck Charlie", the North Korean PO-2 that dropped small bombs and grenades on US Bases.* (Dick Becker)

One of the recurring problems with the F-86 was collapse of the nose wheel while parked. The problem was not with the airplane, as the crew chief just forgot to put the nose gear lock in place. Under the right (or wrong) conditions, the nose wheel could fold up, leaving the F-86 resting on its nose with minimal damage. This photo clearly shows the lack of a pitot tube on the right wingtip. (Tom Foote)

COs of the 15th TRS at Kimpo, and Capt. Joe Daley, Operations Officer of the 15th, made a determined effort to get a recon version of the F-86 somehow, some way. First they obtained a Class 26d F-86 forward fuselage from the boneyard at Kimpo. Working in their spare time, they found that by removing the guns and ammo bays, a camera could be installed. Mounted horizontally, the K-25 bomb scoring camera, "liberated" from a B-26 Invader, shot into a small optical mirror set at a 45°, looking through a small hole cut into the bottom of the fuselage. It worked and FEAMCOM authorized the building of two aircraft at the repair facility at Tachikawa.

A pair of war weary F-86As were pulled from the 4th FIG inventory and had the necessary modifications done to mount a single K-25 in the right lower fuselage. It looked exactly like a standard F-86A from the 4th FIG, unless you crawled under the right side and looked up. The fuselage was not bulged in any way. The entire left

Miss Behaving, an F-86A-5 assigned to Lt. Don Torres in the 334th FIS, on the ramp at K-14 in the Summer of 1951. Miss Behaving was also flown to victory by Capt. Dick Becker, who got credit for two MiG kills flying Torres' F-86A. The open gun bay door was used as the first step in entering the cockpit. (Don Torres)

WARBIRD**TECH**
S E R I E S

- Guns are bore sighted parallel to the fuselage reference line and centerline.

- The gun sight line is bore sighted down to intersect the mean gun bore at 750 yards for gun firing.

- The A-1CM sight with the rocket setting unit provides a gun sight depression angle of 3 degrees 53 minutes from the fuselage reference line for rocket firing. Rocket bore sighting is accomplished by setting the rocket setting unit to "5" HVAR-N." Depress and hold electrical caging button while adjusting cam follower (inside rocket setting unit) to give a sight line of 47-1/2 mils below fuselage reference line (16-1/2 inches on target board).

- The A-1C(M-1) gun sight with a variable-sight selector unit provides a gun sight depression angle of 2 degrees 12 minutes from the fuselage reference line for rocket firing. Rocket bore sighting is accomplished by setting the variable-sight selector unit to "ROCKET" and the rocket depression angle pointer to 17 mils. Depress and hold electrical caging button while adjusting bore-sight adjustment ("B.S. ADJ.") screw on face of sight selector to give a sight line of 34-1/2 mils below fuselage reference line (3-13/16 inches on target board).

- The A-4 sight with a fixed sight selector also provides a gun sight depression angle of 3 degrees 53 minutes from the fuselage reference line for rocket firing. Rocket bore sighting is accomplished by setting the fixed sight selector to "ROCKET" and "5" HVAR-N." Depress and hold electrical caging button while adjusting bore-sight adjustment ("B. S. ADJ.") screw on face of fixed sight selector to give a sight line of 47-1/2 mils below fuselage reference line (16-1/2 inches on target board).

- The A-4 sight with a variable sight selector provides a gun sight depression angle of 2 degrees 12 minutes from the fuselage reference line for rocket firing. Rocket bore sighting is accomplished by setting the variable sight selector unit to "ROCKET" and the rocket depression angle pointer to 17 mils. Depress and hold electrical caging button while adjusting bore-sight adjustment ("B. S. ADJ.") screw on face of sight selector to give a sight line of 34-1/2 mils below fuselage reference line (3-13/16 inches on target board).

- Gun sight computer is installed level ($\pm\frac{1}{2}$ degree) to fuselage reference line.

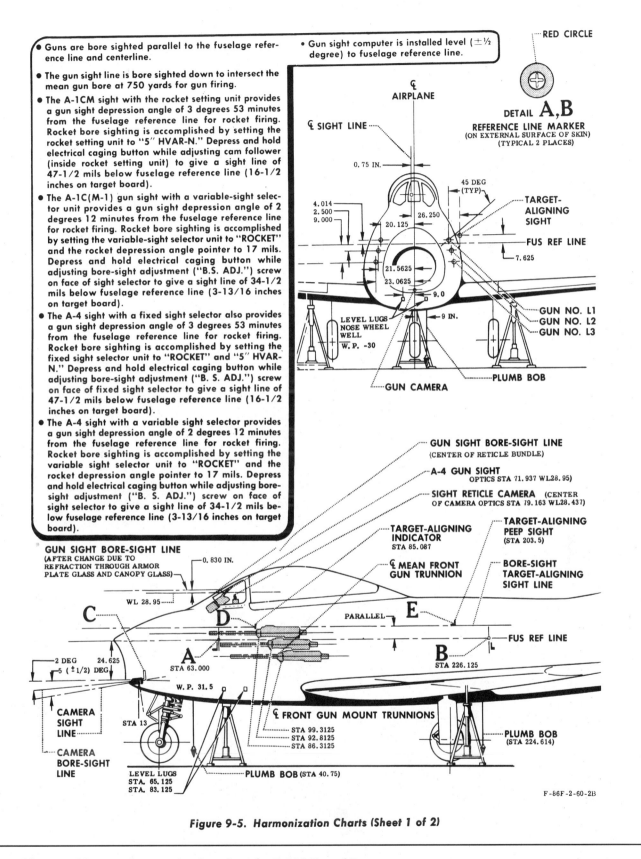

Figure 9-5. Harmonization Charts (Sheet 1 of 2)

F-86F-2-60-2B

.50 calibre machine gun harmonization chart for F-86A, E, and F

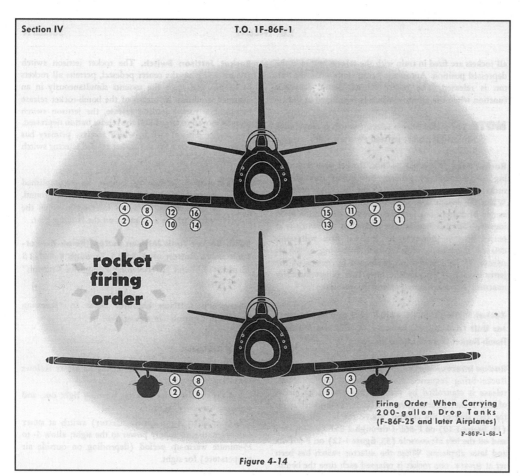

rocket firing order

④ ⑧ ⑫ ⑯   ⑮ ⑪ ⑦ ③
② ⑥ ⑩ ⑭   ⑬ ⑨ ⑤ ①

④ ⑧   ⑦ ③
② ⑥   ⑤ ①

Firing Order When Carrying
200-gallon Drop Tanks
(F-86F-25 and later Airplanes)

F-86F-1-68-1

Figure 4-14

F-86A, E, or F rocket firing order.

TRAY airplanes were again drawn from war weary F-86As serving with the 4th at Kimpo. One of the problems with the HONEYBUCKET aircraft was blurred photos caused by vibration of the mirror. FEAMCOM and the men from the 15th TRS revised and insulated the mirror assembly to reduce vibration. They also mounted the larger K-9 camera in place of the K-25. And two of the K-9s would be used. This involved emptying both gun bays and bulging the underside of the fuselage, giving the ASHTRAY airplanes a "chipmunk cheek" appearance.

gun bay area remained intact, and the right gun compartment still had the upper two guns operational. These two aircraft were known as HONEYBUCKETs. Capt. Daley brought the first HONEYBUCKET back to Kimpo in October 1951. The pilots of the HONEYBUCKET Sabre's flew as #4 in a four ship flight of 4th FIG Sabres. The aircraft were even parked on the 4th FIG side of the runway.

The normal nose "art" found on F-86s of the 4th FIG was a simple name. Miss Kumsum Mo was assigned to the 335th FIS. Note that it still carries the black rudder stripe left over from the black and white ID band markings. The aircraft is also carrying a pair of the 165 gallon drop tanks developed from the Misawa F-80 tanks. (Bob Makinney)

Although the HONEYBUCKET conversions did the job, it was barely adequate. More cameras were required for the mission to be completely successful. Project ASHTRAY was initiated. The 8 additional ASH-

The ASHTRAY conversions were literally hand built at Tachikawa. As such, each was different from the others. Some had a K-9 dicing camera mounted in the upper nose, formerly occupied by the APG-5C

WARBIRD**TECH**
S E R I E S

Lt. Col. Glenn T. Eagleston's F-86A prior to his engagement with "Casey Jones" in June 1951. It carries the full markings seen on aircraft of the 334th FIS—winged star which sometimes carried the crew chief's name, black and white ID bands on fuselage and wings, and black rudder stripe. Under the canopy is a miniature 334th "Pigeon" emblem. The nose cone is natural fiberglass brown, not painted red. (Larry Davis)

radar. Some retained the upper pair of .50 caliber guns, while others had no armament at all. All the camera controls in the cockpit, were mounted on the former bomb/rocket selector panel. In addition to the 8 "new" ASHTRAY RF-86As, the original HONEYBUCKET aircraft were also brought up to ASHTRAY specifications. After a successful mission during the Korean War, the RF-86As were replaced first by HAYMAKER RF-86F conversion, then by North American-built RF-86Fs, which were in turn replaced with RF-84F Thunderflash photo recon aircraft. The RF-86As went to the 115th FIS/California ANG, where they were returned to the air to air combat mission.

Several F-86As line the ramp at K-14 during the Summer of 1951. By this date, there were still only two squadrons flying combat operations, with aircraft coming from a "pool" taken from all three squadrons. Thus a flight could have aircraft from all three squadrons, and pilots as well. The B-29 under tarps in the back, was the "engine repair shop" for the 4th FIG at Kimpo in the Summer of 1951! (Larry Davis)

F-86E & THE "ALL-FLYING TAIL"

The next aircraft in the Sabre series was the F-86E (NA-170). The initial production run of sixty F-86E-1s (50-579/-638) were virtually identical to the last twenty four F-86A-5s, with the type A-1CM gun sight and AN/APG-30 ranging radar, and the J47-GE-13 engine rated at 5430 lbs. of thrust. However, there was one difference between the A and the E-1 that would change the flight envelope of the F-86 forever. It had been found during testing of the XP-86 and F-86A, that something happened to the flight controls as the aircraft speed entered the transonic speed ranges. The controls lost their effectiveness and suffered what is referred to as "control reversal," i.e., if you tried to go up using normal control functions, you continued to go down!

The problem was that air loads over the elevators were too great to

F-579-CHASE AIRPLANE   3-19-55   202-92-9C

The #1 F-86E gaudily painted as a chase plane in 1955. The F-86E was the first the have the "all-flying tail" assembly, which allowed both the front and rear of the horizontal stabilizer to move up and down, creating almost three times the surface for air flow to work on than was found on the F-86A. (NAA)

42

main differences table

F-86 SERIES ITEM	A	D, K, AND L	E	F	H
	F-86A	F-86D, K, AND L	F-86E	F-86F	F-86H
Engine	J47-GE-7 or -13	J47-GE-17, -17B, or -33 with afterburner	J47-GE-13	J47-GE-27	J73-GE-3 Series
Engine Control	Mechanical	Electronic	Mechanical	Mechanical	Hydromechanical
Automatic Pilot	No	Yes	No	No	No
Horizontal Tail	Conventional	Single, controllable surface	Controllable stabilizer and elevator	Controllable stabilizer and elevator	Controllable stabilizer and elevator
Aileron & Horizontal Tail Control	Conventional and hydraulic boost	Full-power hydraulic irreversible control	Full-power hydraulic irreversible control	Full-power hydraulic irreversible control	Full-power hydraulic irreversible control
Aileron & Horizontal Tail Artificial Feel System	No	Yes	Yes	Yes	Yes
Armament	Machine guns, bombs, rockets, or chemical tanks	F-86D AND F-86L: Rockets in fuselage package F-86K: 20mm guns	Machine guns, bombs, rockets, or chemical tanks	Machine guns, bombs, rockets, or special store	Machine guns, bombs, rockets, or special store
Windshield	"V"	Flat	"V" or flat	Flat	Flat
Canopy Ejection Control	Right handgrip on seat Either handgrip (some airplanes)	Either handgrip on seat	Right handgrip on seat Either handgrip (some airplanes)	Either handgrip on seat	Either handgrip on seat
Canopy	Sliding	Clamshell	Sliding	Sliding	Clamshell
Oxygen Regulator	A-14 or D-2	D-1, D-2, D-2A, or MD-1	A-14 or D-2	D-1, D-2, or D-2A	D-2

F-86F-1-00-66C

Figure 1-2

Changed 27 October 1961

F-86Es ready for final assembly at Inglewood in early 1951. The Es, with their all-flying tail assembly, were rushed into production in early 1951 and sent to Korea to give American pilots another advantage against the MiG. (USAF)

be overcome by the hydraulically boosted controls used on the F-86A. This could be overcome in a couple of different ways—by increasing the dimensions of the elevator or increase the amount of hydraulic boost that operated the elevators. North American chose to do both. But they also wanted to do

An element of F-86Es from the 33rd FIG based at Otis AFB, Massachusetts. The first E models delivered to the Air Force went to the 33rd, serving as service test aircraft as well as being combat ready. As soon as the 33rd had enough aircraft to equip one squadron, Air Force began sending F-86Es to the Korean Theater. (USAF)

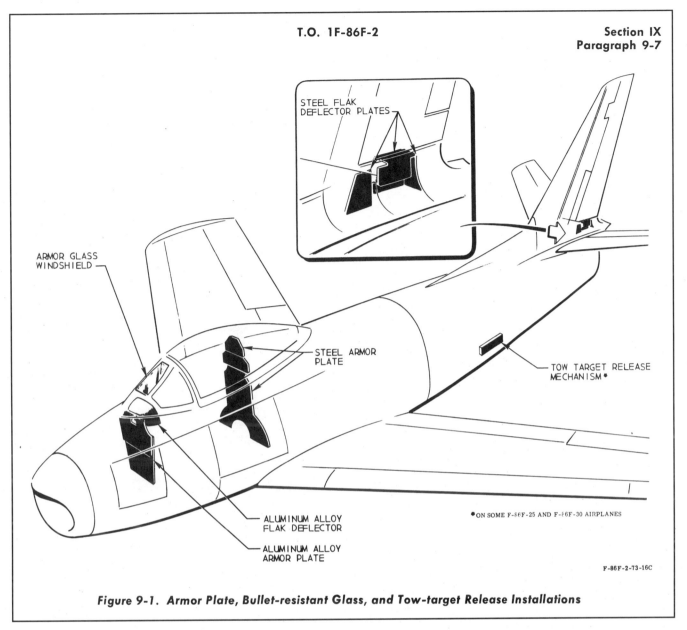

Figure 9-1. Armor Plate, Bullet-resistant Glass, and Tow-target Release Installations

Drawing showing the armor plated area around the pilot of the F-86E/F. Note that there were special flak plates around the "all-flying tail" mechanism. The guns on the sides of the cockpit were a very good flak and cannon deflector shield.

it without increasing the size of the elevator or compromising the pilot's feel of the controls. North American's engineers increased the size of the elevator by making the the fixed stabilizer portion movable. The movable stabilizer was geared to the movement of the elevators, creating a greater angle of attack for the elevator surfaces to act upon. As the elevator moved up, the stabilizer leading edge moved

Everything was tried to increase the range of the F-86, including modified underwing fuel tanks with probes, which could plug in to the refueling

drogue of KB-29 tankers. This F-86E was one of two test aircraft for Air Proving Ground at Eglin AFB. (W.J. Balogh, Sr.)

Miss B was one of the first F-86Es to reach the 51st FIG at Suwon AB in September 1951. The 51st FIG had been flying Lockheed F-80C Shooting Stars, but transitioned into the brand new F-86E when the MiG threat started to escalate in late summer 1951. The early F-86Es still had the fiberglass nose cone as found on F-86As. (USAF)

down, and vice versa. Thus was created the so-called "all-flying tail."

In conjunction with the "all-flying tail," North American's engineers gave the system full hydraulic, power-operated flight controls that would assure complete maneuverability throughout all the speed ranges. But this "irreversible flight control system" also gave the pilot no sense of "feel" in the controls.

These 51st FIG crew chiefs are about to remove the tail-pipe plug from an F-86E-10 in the Spring of 1952. Both intake and exhausts were "plugged" whenever the aircraft weren't flying to keep Korean "friendlies" from throwing rocks and other debris into the engine. The aircraft has had some type of fuselage repair, as the buzz number is a non-standard font. (USAFM)

WARBIRDTECH
SERIES

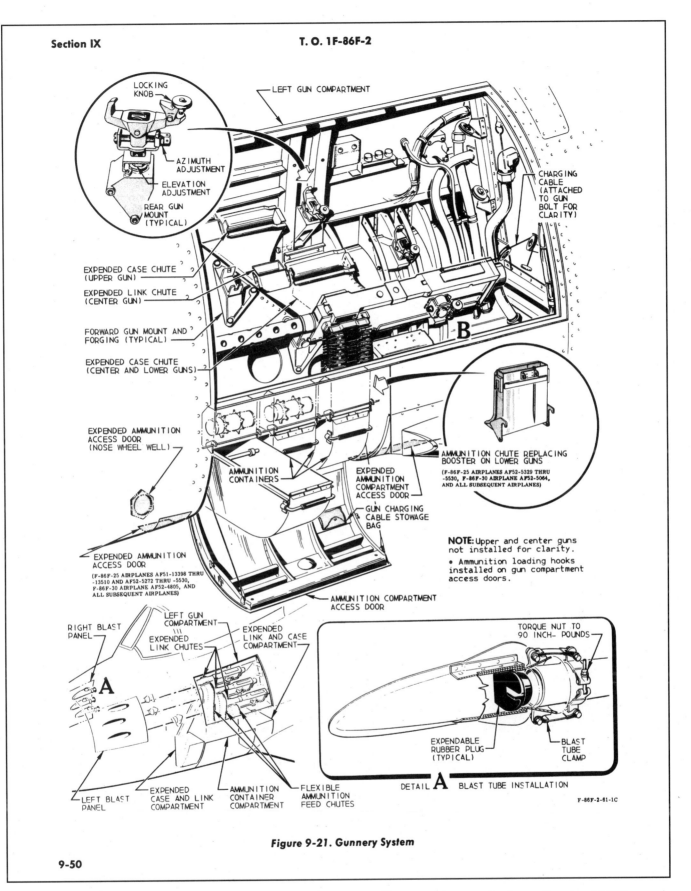

LOCKING
KNOB

AZIMUTH
ADJUSTMENT

ELEVATION
ADJUSTMENT

REAR GUN
MOUNT
(TYPICAL)

LEFT GUN COMPARTMENT

CHARGING
CABLE
(ATTACHED
TO GUN
BOLT FOR
CLARITY)

EXPENDED CASE CHUTE
(UPPER GUN)

EXPENDED LINK CHUTE
(CENTER GUN)

FORWARD GUN MOUNT AND
FORGING (TYPICAL)

EXPENDED CASE CHUTE
(CENTER AND LOWER GUNS)

EXPENDED AMMUNITION
ACCESS DOOR
(NOSE WHEEL WELL)

AMMUNITION
CONTAINERS

EXPENDED
AMMUNITION
COMPARTMENT
ACCESS DOOR

GUN CHARGING
CABLE STOWAGE
BAG

AMMUNITION CHUTE REPLACING
BOOSTER ON LOWER GUNS
(F-86F-25 AIRPLANES AF52-5329 THRU
-5530, F-86F-30 AIRPLANE AF52-5064,
AND ALL SUBSEQUENT AIRPLANES)

EXPENDED AMMUNITION
ACCESS DOOR
(F-86F-25 AIRPLANES AF51-13398 THRU
-13510 AND AF52-5272 THRU -5530,
F-86F-30 AIRPLANE AF52-4805, AND
ALL SUBSEQUENT AIRPLANES)

AMMUNITION COMPARTMENT
ACCESS DOOR

NOTE: Upper and center guns
not installed for clarity.
• Ammunition loading hooks
installed on gun compartment
access doors.

RIGHT BLAST
PANEL

LEFT GUN
COMPARTMENT

EXPENDED
LINK CHUTES

EXPENDED
LINK AND CASE
COMPARTMENT

TORQUE NUT TO
90 INCH- POUNDS

LEFT BLAST
PANEL

EXPENDED
CASE AND LINK
COMPARTMENT

AMMUNITION
CONTAINER
COMPARTMENT

FLEXIBLE
AMMUNITION
FEED CHUTES

EXPENDABLE
RUBBER PLUG
(TYPICAL)

DETAIL A BLAST TUBE INSTALLATION

BLAST
TUBE
CLAMP

F-86F-2-61-1C

Figure 9-21. Gunnery System

This drawing shows the gun bay area of the F-86. Each M3 .50 caliber machine gun had a cyclic rate of 1100 rounds per minute. Each ammunition container could hold up to 300 rounds, but a normal mission called for 267 rounds.

NORTH AMERICAN F-86
SabreJet DAY FIGHTERS

The engineers built an artificial "feel" into the controls that gave the pilot the same "feel" to the control stick that he would have if they weren't power-operated. It's sort of like driving a car with variable-ratio power steering. Externally, the F-86E-1 had a large fairing on the rear fuselage, directly in front of the stabilizer, that housed the gearing and hydraulic controls of the "all-flying tail." On September 23rd 1950, the first F-86E-1 (50-579) took to the air for the first time. The Air Force took delivery of its first two E-1s on February 9th 1951. A second batch of fifty one aircraft having minor internal modifications were desig-

Jimmie Boy II, an F-86E-10 from the 51st FIG, on the alert pad at Suwon (K-13) in the summer of 1952. The E-10 had the new flat armored windscreen and metal nose cone. At all times during combat operations, four F-86s were on "alert," in case MiGs attempted to follow the mission aircraft back. (James Kumpf)

Two 25th FIS armorers work on the F-86E flown by Maj. William Whisner, who is credited with 5½ MiGs, two with the 4th FIG and 3½ with the 51st. Whisner was one of a cadre of pilots transferred from the 4th to the 51st to ease the transition from F-80 to F-86. (USAF)

nated F-86E-5 (50-639/-689).

Initially, the production of the E-1s was slated to go to various Air Defense Command units in the United States. Many of these units had been stripped of the best A models when the 4th FIG had deployed to Korea in November 1950. The first unit to receive F-86E-1s was the 33rd FIG at Otis AFB beginning in May 1951. But combat in Korea dictated other needs for the new model Es. As soon as the first squadron of E-1s was operational with the 33rd FIG, production aircraft were diverted to Korea, where the fighting was starting to take a toll. Brand new E-1s and E-5s were loaded aboard the escort carriers USS Cape Esperance and USS

Sitkoh Bay for transport to Korea.

On their arrival in Japan, the new E models were divided up between the veteran MiG-hunters of the 4th FIG at Kimpo, and the 51st FIG at Suwon equipped with the F-80C Shooting Star. An increase in MiG numbers and activity had forced the Far East Air Force (FEAF) to

begin operation of a second F-86 group. Beginning in September 1951, the 51st FIG stood down their aging Lockheed Shooting Stars to begin conversion training in the brand new F-86E Sabre. By December 1951, Colonel Frances "Gabby" Gabreski had his two squadrons, the 16th FIS and 25th FIS, operational over the Yalu River,

Several F-86Es from the 25th FIS line the ramp at K-13 in the late Fall of 1952. The second aircraft in the lineup, This'll Kill Ya, aka Lady Margaret, is the F-86E that set the World Speed Record, proving that records set by Sabres were with production aircraft, not specially prepared record setters. (NAA)

4th FIG crew chiefs carry 165 gallon Misawa tanks to a waiting 336th FIS F-86E at Kimpo in April 1953. The Beech-built underwing fuel tanks were based on the modified Misawa tanks used on F-80Cs. Revetments at K-14 were much higher and longer than those at K-13, partly due to more attacks by "Bedcheck Charlie." (USAF)

claiming twenty five MiGs destroyed during that first month of combat.

Next off the North American assembly line was the F-86E-10 (51-2718/-2849). Originally designed to accept the still more powerful J47-GE-27 engine rated at 5910 lbs of thrust, the E-10s came off the assembly line still powered with the -13 engine as on previous models. Problems in production of the -27 engine held it back until the F-86F series. The E-10 introduced the flat armored windscreen in place of the V-shaped windscreen seen on A-5s and earlier E models. Other changes found on the E-10 included a new gauge layout to the instrument panel, with some different controls and switches in the cockpit. Delivery of the first F-86E-10, #51-2718, came in September 1951, with many being rushed to

Peacemaker, an F-86E-6 flown by Capt. William Champion with the 334th FIS in 1952. The F-86E-6 was one of sixty aircraft built by Canadair Ltd. and purchased by the USAF to augment the dwindling inventories of F-86s in Korea. It was, quite simply, a license-built copy of the F-86E-1 with the V-shaped windscreen. (Curt Francom)

the combat units in Korea. As more and more E models became available, FEAF added a third squadron to the 51st FIG, when they transferred the veteran F-51D equipped 39th FBS from the 18th FBG on June 1st 1952.

There was one E model produced in quantity for the US Air Force—but not by North American Aviation. Canadair Ltd. had had a long association with North American Aviation through the war years, having license-built the AT-6 Texan for use by Royal Canadian and Royal Air Force training programs. They were very interested in building Sabre aircraft for the RCAF, as well as for export sales to other NATO countries. Canadair purchased a single F-86A-5, 49-1069, and had it flown to their factory at Cartierville near Montreal. The aircraft was disassembled and modified to accept the Avro Orenda engine rated at over 6,000 lbs. of thrust. This single aircraft carried the designation of F-86J by North American, but was known as the CL-13 Mk. I by Canadair. It was the prototype for the true Canadair Sabre series.

Tail-pipe segments, commonly known as "rats" or "mice," were inserted into the tail-pipe opening to reduce the area, thus increasing the exhaust temperature. Any increase in exhaust temperature increased thrust and gave the pilot an added couple of miles per hour on top speed.

Capt. James Horowitz (his pen name was James Salter) wrote a book about Korean Sabre operations titled The Hunters, *which was made into a movie starring Robert Mitchum in 1958. Capt. Horowitz flew* Slow Boat to China, *denoted by the flags under the gun panel, one of the early F-86E-1s.* (Karl Dittmer)

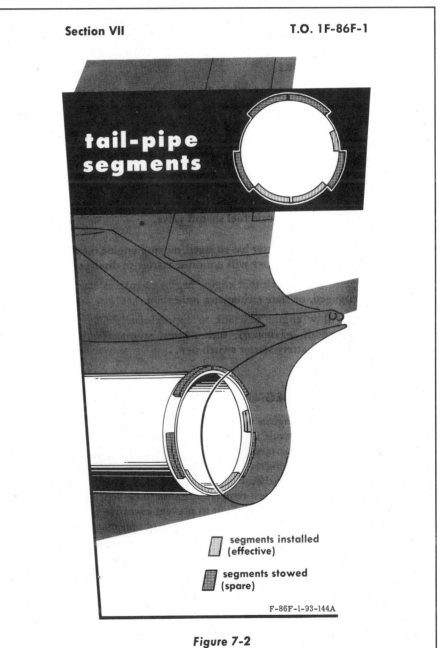

Section VII   T.O. 1F-86F-1

tail-pipe segments

▥ segments installed (effective)

▦ segments stowed (spare)

F-86F-1-93-144A

Figure 7-2

My Hutch, was one of the F-86Es assigned to Tiger Flight in the 25th FIS at K-13. Tiger Flight aircraft had sharks teeth painted on the nose. In the late summer of 1952, the 51st adopted the 12" black checks on the vertical fin as their group marking, with a small color stripe atop the checks as the squadron ID band—blue for the 16th, red for the 25th, and yellow for the 39th FIS. The badge under the windscreen is the 25th FIS. (Larry Davis)

But Canadair also license-built three hundred fifty CL-13 Sabre Mk. 2s, which were identical to North American Aviation-built F-86E-1s, with the "all-flying tail," irreversible flying controls, V-shaped windscreen, and J47-GE-13 engine. The first aircraft off the Canadair assembly line began to equip RCAF squadrons in late 1951. But USAF Sabre inventories, especially in the combat zone, were becoming critically low, and North American's single plant at Inglewood was hard pressed to keep up with demand. The US Air Force then ordered sixty CL-13 Sabre Mk. 2s from Canadair, designated F-86E-6 by the US Air Force.

Flown from Canadair to the North American facility at Fresno, California, the E-6s (52-2833/—2892) were first equipped with USAF radios and other equipment needed in combat, then rushed to Korea during the late Spring of 1952. They were divided between the two Sabre groups flying combat. Following the end of the war, the E-6s

Kimpo AB, Korea, 1953—a 4th FIG F-86E-10 with its aft section removed so that mechanics have access to the engine. Specially designed mobile cradles were used to remove the aft section, which was held on to the forward fuselage with four bolts. Much of the mechanical work was done on the open ramps in Korea under some of the harshest conditions. (Larry Davis)

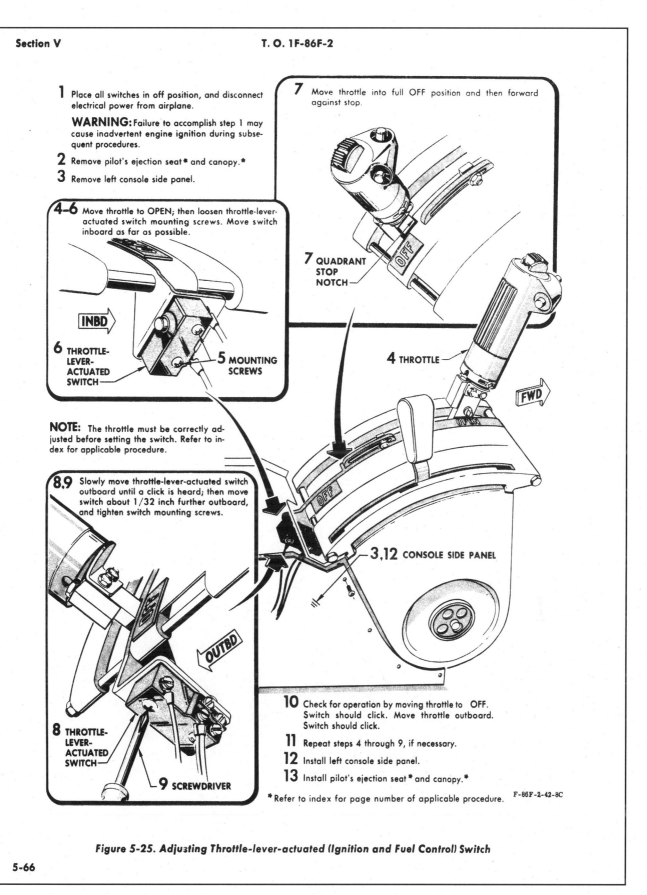

1 Place all switches in off position, and disconnect electrical power from airplane.

WARNING: Failure to accomplish step 1 may cause inadvertent engine ignition during subsequent procedures.

2 Remove pilot's ejection seat* and canopy.*

3 Remove left console side panel.

4-6 Move throttle to OPEN; then loosen throttle-lever-actuated switch mounting screws. Move switch inboard as far as possible.

INBD ➤

6 THROTTLE-LEVER-ACTUATED SWITCH

5 MOUNTING SCREWS

NOTE: The throttle must be correctly adjusted before setting the switch. Refer to index for applicable procedure.

8,9 Slowly move throttle-lever-actuated switch outboard until a click is heard; then move switch about 1/32 inch further outboard, and tighten switch mounting screws.

8 THROTTLE-LEVER-ACTUATED SWITCH

9 SCREWDRIVER

◀ OUTBD

7 Move throttle into full OFF position and then forward against stop.

7 QUADRANT STOP NOTCH

4 THROTTLE

FWD ➤

3,12 CONSOLE SIDE PANEL

10 Check for operation by moving throttle to OFF. Switch should click. Move throttle outboard. Switch should click.

11 Repeat steps 4 through 9, if necessary.

12 Install left console side panel.

13 Install pilot's ejection seat* and canopy.*

* Refer to index for page number of applicable procedure.

F-86F-2-42-8C

Figure 5-25. Adjusting Throttle-lever-actuated (Ignition and Fuel Control) Switch

5-66

The throttle quadrant of the F-86 controlled many things other than the engine, including the speed brakes and microphone.

This F-86E-6, #52-2886, assigned to the US Air Force Academy in August 1956, is a Korean veteran of the 336th FIS at Kimpo. Many of the Canadair-built E-6s went to the Michigan ANG, but many others found their way into special units like the Academy flight. (Bob Esposito)

were transferred to the US Air National Guard, with many of the aircraft finding their way into the Michigan ANG.

The last F-86E came off the North Amer-

Nose art on 4th FIG aircraft flourished from late 1952 through the end of the war. El Diablo was an F-86E-10 assigned to Capt. Chuck Owens in the 336th FIS. The multiple names found on 4th FIG Sabres were supplied by various crew members, a crew chief painted a name on, a pilot did the same, sometimes even the armorer named the airplane. Note the fifteen truck kills and one tank, in addition to eight MiGs claimed. (Lt. Col. William K. Thomas)

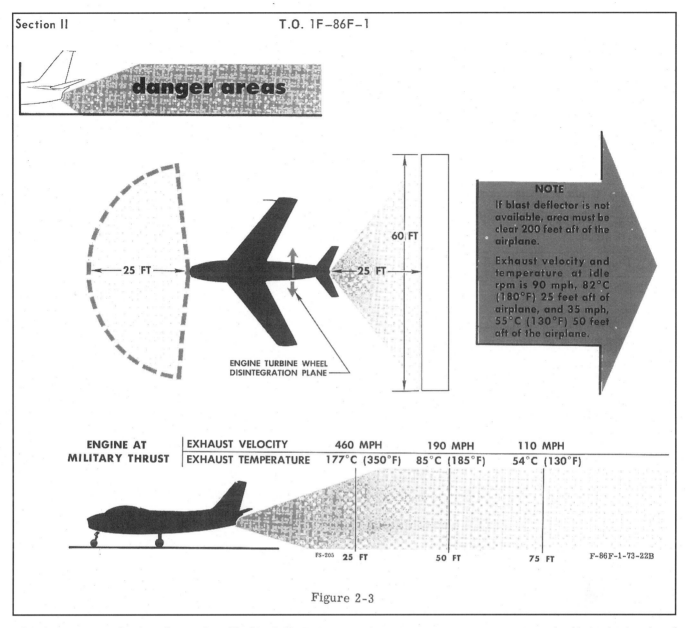

danger areas

60 FT

25 FT

25 FT

NOTE

If blast deflector is not available, area must be clear 200 feet aft of the airplane.

Exhaust velocity and temperature at idle rpm is 90 mph, 82°C (180°F) 25 feet aft of airplane, and 35 mph, 55°C (130°F) 50 feet aft of the airplane.

ENGINE TURBINE WHEEL DISINTEGRATION PLANE

ENGINE AT MILITARY THRUST	EXHAUST VELOCITY	460 MPH	190 MPH	110 MPH
	EXHAUST TEMPERATURE	177°C (350°F)	85°C (185°F)	54°C (130°F)

FS-205   25 FT   50 FT   75 FT   F-86F-1-73-22B

Figure 2-3

The danger areas both in front of and behind the F-86. More than one unwary person was sucked into the intake of an idling jet aircraft, killing them almost instantly.

ican assembly line in October 1952, interspersed with F-86F aircraft. But it was more an accident than a purpose-built F-86E. The production of the F-86E was intended to halt following the E-5 series. But production of the -27 engine forced North American to build an additional one hundred thirty two F-86E-

Four 336th FIS crew chiefs watch the skies for the return of the mission aircraft to Kimpo. The F-86E under wraps is Patricia, *the airplane that Capt. Cliff Jolley flew when he made ace. The tarps covering the aircraft are specially made for the F-86, and cover the entire nose and intake, plus all the upper surfaces of the wings and tailplanes. (Larry Davis)*

The Newark Fireball *was the F-86E assigned to Lt. Henry Cresibene with the 335th FIS. Much of the nose art applied to 4th FIG Sabres was done by Capt. Karl Dittmer, a pilot in the 335th FIS. Note that sitting on the ramp allowed the hydraulically actuated nose gear door and main landing gear doors to "bleed down," while gravity did the same thing with the leading edge slats.* (Henry Cresibene)

Honest John *was the F-86E originally assigned to Col. Walker Mahurin, the commander of the 4th FIG in 1952 before he was shot down and taken prisoner. Col. Mahurin was another ace in the legendary 56th FG during WWII, and now commanding a unit in Korea.* (Lt. Col. William K. Thomas)

Wyoming Thunder, an F-86E-10 flown by Maj Elmer "Hap" Harris with the 25th FIS at K-13 in early 1952. The two squadrons of the 51st FIG, with Col. Francis "Gabby" Gabreski in command, were combat ready in less than two months, flying their first mission on December 1st 1951. (Don Porter)

10s. Problems with -27 engine availability arose again after F-86F production was well underway. After building one hundred thirty five F-86Fs, Air Force authorized North American to re-introduce the -13 engine into the F-86F airframe, which by this time, was already into the F-86F-15 series. The last ninety three F-15s on a one hundred airplane contract, were powered by J47-GE-13 engines, and designated F-86E-15 (51-12977/-13069). The airframe had all the improvements called for in the F-86F series, including the strengthened wing with additional underwing hard points.

The fuselage was designed so that the -27 engine could be installed, if and when they became available. The new, simpler type A-4 gun sight and AN/APG-30 ranging radar was installed, both items were standard F-86F equipment. So closely matched were the E-15s to the F-86Fs, that many were later modified with the "6-3 hard wing," without slats, which was introduced during production of the F-25 and F-30 series. No F-86E-15s went to Korea, most of them going directly to Air National Guard Squadrons right off the assembly line. North American produced three hundred thirty six F-86Es, plus the sixty purchased from Canadair, brought the total of F-86E aircraft accepted by the US Air Force to three hundred ninety six.

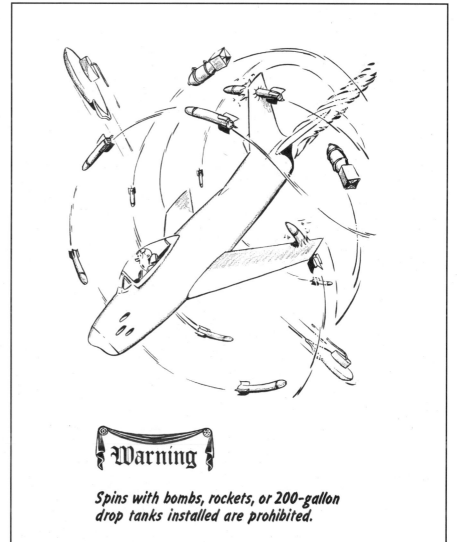

Warning

Spins with bombs, rockets, or 200-gallon drop tanks installed are prohibited.

F-86F SERIES

MiG-KILLER SUPREME

The F-86F was destined to be the ultimate in Sabre design. It started out as merely an updated F-86E having the J47-GE-27 engine rated at 6090 lbs. of thrust. The first seventy eight F-86F-1s on the contract were, in fact, F-86E-10s with the -27 engine. With the more powerful -27 engine, the F-86F was now almost the equal to the MiG-15 in two very important categories—rate of climb and service ceiling. The rate of climb jumped over 2500 ft./min. to 9850 ft./min. in the F-86F-1. This was very close to the MiG's 10,100 ft./min. rate. The service ceiling went to 49,100 feet, which brought the Sabre closer to the MiG's 55,000 feet

Maj. C.L. Hewitt accepts the first F-86F (51-2850) from J.S. Smithson, the Inglewood plant manager. Before production was halted, two North American plants would build 2540 F-86Fs. The first F-86F differed from previous models in having the J47-GE-27 engine rated at 5910 lbs. of thrust. (USAF)

F-86F-30s lined up on the ramp at Inglewood ready for delivery to Air Force squadrons around the world. These production aircraft have the "6-3 wing" with a fence at 70% of the wing span. Although the F-25 is usually credited with being the big MiG-killer in Korea, it was actually the F-30. They just looked like an F-25. Actually, very few F-25s went to Korea at all. (Peter Bowers)

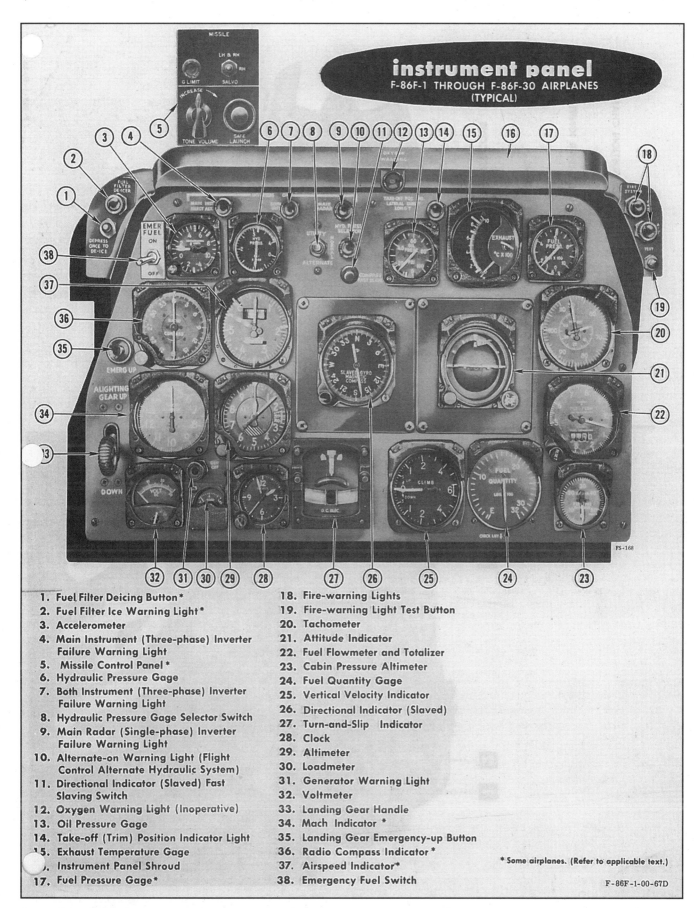

instrument panel
F-86F-1 THROUGH F-86F-30 AIRPLANES
(TYPICAL)

1. Fuel Filter Deicing Button*
2. Fuel Filter Ice Warning Light*
3. Accelerometer
4. Main Instrument (Three-phase) Inverter Failure Warning Light
5. Missile Control Panel *
6. Hydraulic Pressure Gage
7. Both Instrument (Three-phase) Inverter Failure Warning Light
8. Hydraulic Pressure Gage Selector Switch
9. Main Radar (Single-phase) Inverter Failure Warning Light
10. Alternate-on Warning Light (Flight Control Alternate Hydraulic System)
11. Directional Indicator (Slaved) Fast Slaving Switch
12. Oxygen Warning Light (Inoperative)
13. Oil Pressure Gage
14. Take-off (Trim) Position Indicator Light
15. Exhaust Temperature Gage
16. Instrument Panel Shroud
17. Fuel Pressure Gage*

18. Fire-warning Lights
19. Fire-warning Light Test Button
20. Tachometer
21. Attitude Indicator
22. Fuel Flowmeter and Totalizer
23. Cabin Pressure Altimeter
24. Fuel Quantity Gage
25. Vertical Velocity Indicator
26. Directional Indicator (Slaved)
27. Turn-and-Slip   Indicator
28. Clock
29. Altimeter
30. Loadmeter
31. Generator Warning Light
32. Voltmeter
33. Landing Gear Handle
34. Mach Indicator *
35. Landing Gear Emergency-up Button
36. Radio Compass Indicator *
37. Airspeed Indicator*
38. Emergency Fuel Switch

* Some airplanes. (Refer to applicable text.)

F-86F-1-00-67D

Instrument panel layout of the F-86F.

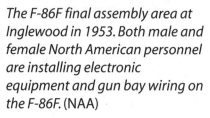

The F-86F final assembly area at Inglewood in 1953. Both male and female North American personnel are installing electronic equipment and gun bay wiring on the F-86F. (NAA)

ceiling. The MiGs could still ride high above the Sabres, but they could no longer use the "Zoom And Sun" tactic to dive down on the F-86s and then zoom climb back to altitude. The top speed of the F-1 was 695 MPH, almost 30 MPH faster than any MiG-15. The F-86F could still not maneuver with the MiGs at combat altitudes, i.e., over 40,000 feet. And the MiGs could still cross the Yalu at above 53,000 feet with impunity. But once they came down "off their perch," they were dead meat in the sights of a veteran Sabre pilot.

The first flight of the F-86F-1 came on March 19th, 1952. Other changes between the F-86E and the F-86F included: incorporating the A-4 gun sight with the AN/APG-30 ranging radar beginning with the F-10; and strengthening the wing so that multiple

Aircraft that were sent to Korea were ferried aboard US Navy aircraft carriers. As such, these Sabres were cocooned with a spray on plastic wrap, which was stripped off on arrival. The first F-86As sent to Korea were covered with cosmoline to retard corrosion. It didn't work and all the aircraft suffered damage and needed repair before being readied for combat. (Larry Davis)

A/2C David Dawson installs an M3 .50 caliber machine gun in a 44th FBS F-86F at Clark AB, The Philippines during July 1954. The empty compartment below the gun bay is where the ammunition containers (3) are installed. Each .50 caliber M3 could fire 1100 rounds/minute. (USAF)

cockpit left side
F-86F-1 THROUGH F-86F-20 AIRPLANES

1. Anti-G Suit Pressure-regulating Valve
2. Circuit-breaker Panel
3. Ammunition Compartment Heat Emergency Shutoff Handle
4. Ammunition Compartment Overheat Warning Light
5. Air Outlet Selector Lever
6. Windshield Anti-icing Overheat Warning Light
7. Console Floodlight
8. Side Air Outlet
9. Windshield Anti-icing Lever
10. Throttle
11. Rocket Intervalometer
12. Canopy and Windshield Auxiliary Defrost Lever
13. Instrument Panel Floodlight and Extension Light Alternate Mounting
14. Console Panel

15. Parking Brake Handle
16. Canopy Switch
17. Instrument Panel Floodlight
18. Emergency Jettison Handle
19. Type D-1 or D-2 Oxygen Regulator Panel
20. Forward Console
21. Throttle Friction Wheel
22. Wing Flap Lever
23. Speed Brake Emergency Lever
24. Flight Control Switch
25. Longitudinal Alternate Trim Switch
26. Rudder Trim Switch
27. Cockpit Pressure Control Switch
28. Lateral Alternate Trim Switch
29. Cockpit Pressure Schedule Selector Switch
30. Cockpit Air Temperature Control Rheostat
31. Aft Console
32. Cockpit Air Temperature Control Switch
33. Drop Tank Pressure Shutoff Valve
34. Extension Light *

*Some airplanes (Refer to applicable text)

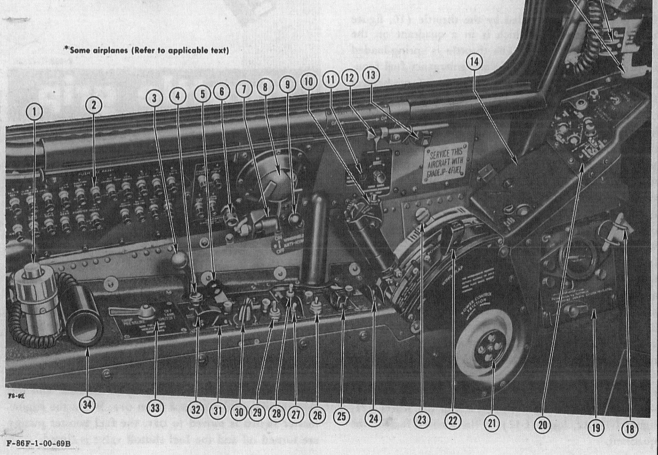

F-86F-1-00-69B

Cockpit layout (left side) of the F-86F.

F-86Fs slated for the fighter bomber mission had canopies with these lines showing the angle of attack. Printed on large pieces of film, the lines could be easily removed. Behind the ejector seat at the aft end of the canopy is the radio compass loop antenna. (NAA)

drop tanks or bombs could be carried beginning with the F-5. The type A-4 gun sight was a much simpler unit than the type A-1CM, making it more reliable. The wing was first strengthened to carry a pair of 1000 lb. bombs or 200 gallon drop tanks. However, beginning with the F-86F-25 and F-30, a second pair of

An F-86F from the 50th FBW at Hahn AB, Germany. Being based close to the Iron Curtain and the MiGs, the 50th FBW Sabres had yellow bands around the wings and fuselage very similar to aircraft in Korea. Note the use of 206.5 gallon drop tanks. (Lt. Col. Pasqualicchio)

1. Stand-by Compass
2. Right Forward Console
3. Spare Bulb Storage
4. Side Air Outlet
5. Instrument Panel Floodlight
6. Side Air Outlet Control Valve
7. Console Floodlight
8. Instrument Panel Floodlight and Extension Light Alternate Mounting
9. Instrument Panel Primary Light Rheostat
10. Instrument Panel Auxiliary Light Rheostat
11. Console and Panel Light Rheostat

12. Circuit-breaker Panel
13. Map Case
14. Extension Light*
15. Sight Ground Test Plug
16. IFF Control Panel *
17. Right Aft Console
18. Radio Compass Control Panel*
19. Radio Frequency Card
20. VHF Command Radio Control Panel*
21. Emergency Override Handle (Flight Control Hydraulic System)
22. Canopy Alternate Emergency Jettison Handle

cockpit
right side
F-86F-1 THROUGH F-86F-15
AIRPLANES

*Some airplanes (Refer to applicable text.)

F-86F-1-00-70B

Cockpit layout (right side) of the F-86F.

One of the few units in stateside Air Defense Command to fly the F-86F was the 84th FIS at Hamilton AFB, California in 1954. Within months the 84th would transition into a true all-weather aircraft, Northrop F-89 Scorpions. The nose and tail are painted black and yellow, with a red "sabre" on the nose flash. (NAA)

A trio of 461st FDS F-86Fs over Germany in 1956. Two of the Sabres are painted in an experimental USAF camouflage of NATO green and grey in a random pattern, but with full USAF and 461st FDS markings. The camouflage was never adopted for use. (Larry Davis)

hard points were added outboard of the drop tank pylons. On the second pair of pylons a pair of drop tanks was carried, while the ordnance was carried on the inboard, original pylons. This was the first true fighter bomber Sabre variant. The F-20 added the AN/ARC-33 radio system. The other major change with the F series was a second source of manufacturing. Air Force demand for the F-86F was so great that North American was forced to open a second production line at their Columbus, Ohio facility. The Columbus plant built the F-20 and F-25, while Los (text continued on page 70)

The 388th FBW deployed its aircraft to Etain AB, France in the winter of 1954/55. The 388th remained on duty as part of USAFE until 1957, when they were redesignated the 49th FBW. Unlike transfers to the Far East, these F-86Fs were flown to bases in Europe by way of Greenland, Iceland, England, and then to European bases. (David Menard)

WARBIRD**TECH**
S E R I E S

THE COLORFUL SABRE

The era of the F-86 Sabre was one of the most colorful eras in the history of air warfare. Beginning in the late 1940s, F-86s were adorned with very colorful markings that differentiated each wing or group from one another, and each squadron within a wing. Colorful stripes abounded indicating everything from rank within a flight to command rankings, from flight colors to combat identification colors. And F-86s weren't all natural metal either. Sabres wore every conceivable camouflage scheme from NATO greens and greys to USAF Vietnam tans and greens. And the paint jobs on target towing aircraft were absolutely stunning!

During the Korean War, Sabres were, for the most part, natural metal. There was no anti-corrosion silver or grey paint. and the only "standard" additions to all aircraft were the Far East Air Force (FEAF) recognition bands used for quick identification between a Sabre and a MiG. These were added at the very beginning of Sabre-MiG battles with 4th FIG F-86As and Es having black and white bands painted around the fuselage and wingtips. When the 51st FIG was equipped with F-86Es, they adopted black and yellow ID bands in the same positions as the 4th aircraft. FEAF adopted the black and yellow ID bands as standard for any F-86 aircraft operating in the Korean Theater of Operations, beginning in the summer of 1952. No matter what unit markings were carried on the tail or nose of an F-86, they all had the "standard" FEAF ID bands on the fuselage and wingtips.

Individual markings, especially in Korea, abounded. Nose art was plentiful in the 4th FIG, while simple names were normally found on F-86s of the other units in Korea. Kill markings were either a small red

At least two "factory-built" RF-86F-30s made their way to the war in Korea before it was halted in July 1953. Kneeling on the wing of this 15th TRS RF-86F is Ozzie Niederman, a North American Aviation Tech Rep assigned to the 67th TRW in 1953. The RF-86Fs were painted exactly like their fighter cousins across the field at Kimpo, including painted-on "gun ports." RF-86s often flew as no. 4 in a flight of 4th FIG Sabres. Note mechanic inside engine intake. (Ozzie Niederman)

An F-86F-25 that has been modified to F-40 standards with extended, slatted wings and AIM-9 Sidewinder capabilities, sits on the ramp at Osan AB in July 1976. The SEA camouflaged F-86F was assigned to the 121st Fighter Squadron, Republic of Korea Air Force. ROKAF Sabres served into the 1980s before being phased out in favor of Northrop F-5s. (via Stephen Miller)

star or MiG silhouette under the windscreen. Interestingly, the number of MiG kills was usually different between the left and right side. The amount of MiG kills applied to the left side were those credited to the assigned pilot of the Sabre, while those on the right side were those accumulated by the airplane itself. The same standard was applied to names and art on an F-86, i.e., left side—pilot, right side—crew chief.

Camouflage paint is usually associated with NATO aircraft. But the F-86 was again different from the standard. Of course, RAF, RCAF, Bundesluftwaffe, and other NATO Sabres were often camouflaged in green and grey, with a light blue underside. Several USAFE F-86 squadrons experimented with camouflage schemes based on NATO

One of the more colorful Sabre units was the "Hat In The Ring Squadron," the 94th FIS based at George AFB, California. The yellow lightning bolt markings were applied specifically for a fly-over of President-elect Dwight Eisenhower's inauguration in early 1953, and were retained for the gunnery competition held at Nellis AFB that same summer. (Budd Butcher)

Certainly one of the most colorful markings ever seen on a Sabre were these on a Montana ANG F-86A target tug. These aircraft were outfitted with special reel assemblies to tow a target sleeve or "rag," on which other Sabres would fire live ammunition. Only the fuselage was painted yellow. (P. Paulsen)

This F-86H carries special markings as a Lockheed chase aircraft during the F-104S test program, including Lockheed Starfighter logos on the nose and drop tanks. The aircraft is one of the initial batch of F-86H-1s having six .50 caliber machine gun armament. (Joe Michaels)

colors. In Korea, several F-86As had overall olive drab upper surfaces for a special mission flown only by 4th FIG pilots. And of course, the so-called "SouthEast Asia" camouflage of two greens and a tan, with light grey undersides, was applied to any remaining F-86 squadrons in tactical use within the Air National Guard. During the late 1960s the ROKAF F-86 squadrons, as well as many supplied to Central American air forces were also painted in greens and tans.

But by far, the most colorful aircraft were those assigned target towing duties, commonly called "tugs." These aircraft, by necessity, had to be highly visible to the aircraft that were firing at the target sleeve or rag. Thus they were all very colorfully marked. Many wore overall International Orange on all

The Royal Saudi Air Force was equipped with two squadrons of F-86Fs during the mid-1960s. Based at Jedda, the F-86Fs were all ex-USAF aircraft that were ferried to Saudi Arabia by USAFE pilots following extensive refurbishing. At first the aircraft were painted silver, but later received an overall gloss grey finish. (Brig. Gen. J. Ralph)

The Republic of Korea Air Force had one squadron of twelve RF-86Fs within the 10th Fighter Wing based at Suwon in 1968. The reconnaissance Sabres were standard production RF-86Fs, but having the extended wing installed. This aircraft carries a pair of the 206.5 gallon drop tanks. (Stephen Miller)

A lineup of F-86F-40s from the 8th Fighter Squadron at Komatsu AB in August 1972. The F-86F-40 was a license-built copy of the F-86F built by Mitsubishi Heavy Industries. It was identical to USAF F-86Fs except it had the "6-3 wing" with slats, and the wing tips were extended one foot. Mitsubishi built a total of 300 F-40s, both for JASDF service and other nations. (Hideki Nagakubo)

the upper surfaces. Some were overall yellow. Arizona ANG F-86 tugs had an orange scheme applied to just the uppermost portions of the fuselage and wings, without compromising the ornate Arizona ANG "Copperhead" unit markings.

Between the years 1949 and 1962, US Air Force airplanes carried some of the most colorful markings in aviation history. And the F-86 was one of the most colorful of the colorful.

Another F-86H unit recalled to active duty was the 104th TFS/Maryland ANG, which was recalled during the Pueblo Crisis in 1968. The 104th F-86Hs were already in SEA camouflage, and simply added the tail codes "CT," which meant they were based at Cannon AFB, New Mexico.
(Frank MacSorley)

The Commonwealth CA-27 Sabre 32 was an Australian license-built version of the F-86F, but powered by a Rolls Royce Avon engine with 7500 lbs. of thrust. The CA-27 Sabre had a pair of 30mm Aden cannons in place of the six .50s found in USAF Sabres. This CA-27 was assigned to the Marksmen aerobatic team of No. 2 OCU/Royal Australian Air Force in 1966. (via Stephen Miller)

A Royal Canadian Air Force Sabre Mk. 6 from 430 Squadron, wears the typical NATO green and grey camouflage found on RCAF Sabres in the late 1950s. The aircraft was photographed during an air show at Chambley AB, France in June 1957. RCAF Sabre squadrons stood the line alongside USAFE Sabres against Soviet threats during the Cold War. (via Stephen Miller)

WARBIRD**TECH**
S E R I E S

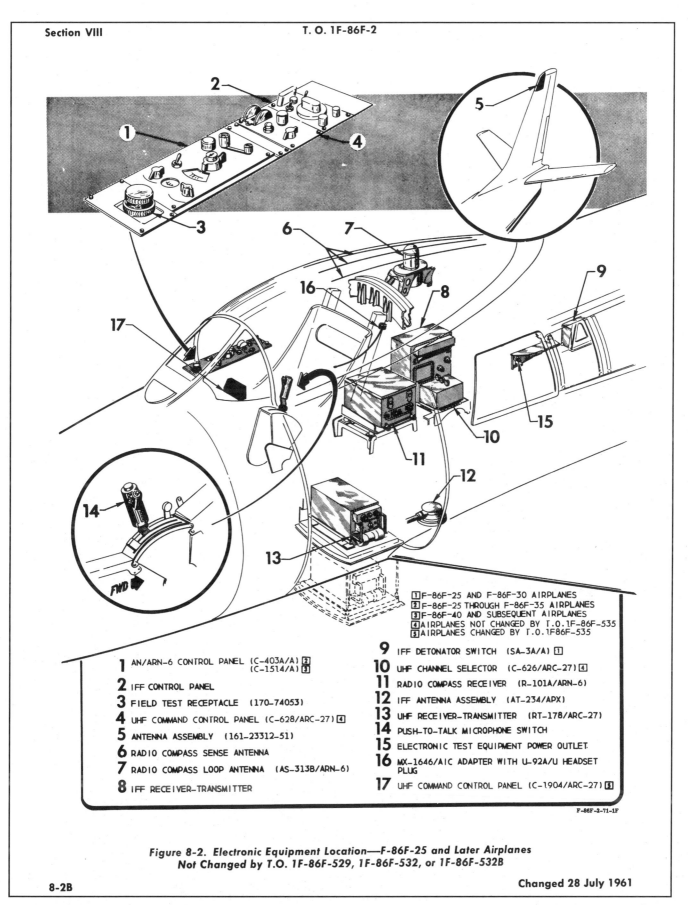

Electronic and radio equipment normally found in an F-86.

NORTH AMERICAN F-86
SABREJET **DAY FIGHTERS**

69

Mechanics work on the engine of Capt. R.W. Blandin's 526th FBS F-86F-25 at Landstuhl AB, Germany in March 1954. The aircraft carries the extra long range 200 gallon combat tanks developed for the F-86 after the end of the Korean War. (Lt. Col. R.W. Blandin)

(text continued from page 64) Angeles built the F-1, F-5, F-10, F-15, F-30 and F-35.

The so-called "6-3 wing" was developed and introduced during

production of the F-25/F-30. Wind tunnel testing indicated that by increasing the size of the wing, coupled with an increase in the angle

of sweep on the wing leading edge, the combat maneuverability could be literally doubled by adding over 1½ Gs to the effective maneuver-

An F-86F from the 391st FBS taxis past other 366th FBW Sabres at Alexandria AFB, Louisiana (now England AFB) in 1956. The aircraft carries special black wing stripes to designate it as one of the aggressor nation aircraft during a war "game." The black and yellow stripes on the nose, vertical and horizontal tail are the unit markings of the 391st FBS. (NAA)

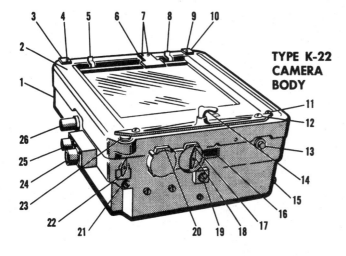

TYPE K-22 CAMERA BODY

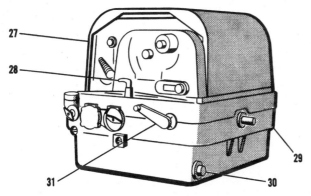

TYPE K-22 AIRCRAFT CAMERA AND A-5A MAGAZINE

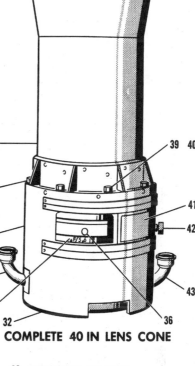

COMPLETE 40 IN LENS CONE

1 CAMERA CASE
2 SHUTTER
3 MAGAZINE RETAINING PLATE
4 RETAINING PLATE SCREW
5 MAGAZINE RETAINER PLUNGER
6 STENCIL PLATE (REF ONLY)
7 STENCIL SCREWS (REF ONLY)
8 MAGAZINE RETAINER PLUNGER
9 RETAINING PLATE SCREW
10 MAGAZINE RETAINING PLATE
11 CLAMP SCREW
12 MAGAZINE LOCK BAR SCREW
13 MANUAL WIND SOCKET
14 MAGAZINE RETAINING LOCK PLUNGER KNOB
15 MANUAL TRIP BUTTON
16 TRIP COUNTER

17 DIAPHRAGM DIAL
18 DIAPHRAGM WIND KNOB
19 DIAPHRAGM REMOTE-CONTROL SHAFT
20 SHUTTER DIAL
21 SHUTTER REMOTE-CONTROL SHAFT
22 SHUTTER WIND KNOB
23 CASE LEVEL
24 POWER SOCKET
25 INTERVALOMETER SOCKET
26 TRUNNION
27 A-5A ROLL FILM MAGAZINE
28 MAGAZINE RETAINING LOCK PLUNGER KNOB
29 CAMERA CASE
30 MANUAL TRIP PLUNGER BUTTON
31 MANUAL WIND HANDLE

32 CONE NOSE ASSEMBLY
33 INDEX ARROW
34 HOSE OUTLET ELBOW ASSEMBLY
35 LENS ASSEMBLY
36 KNURLED KNOB
37 SCREWS
38 LENS AND NOSE ADAPTER
39 LENS MOUNTING SCREWS
40 LOCK WASHERS
41 DIAPHRAGM DOOR
42 LOCK KNOB
43 HOSE INLET ELBOW ASSEMBLY

F-86F-2-73-31

Figure 9-48. K-22 Camera Components

Camera equipment for the RF-86F photo reconnaissance Sabre.

NORTH AMERICAN F-86
SABREJET DAY FIGHTERS

F-86Fs from the 512th Fighter Day Squadron, i.e. air superiority mission, taxi to their parking ramp at Soesterberg AB, The Netherlands in November 1954. The 512th FDS, a squadron within the 406th FDW at RAF Manston, was the first USAF unit stationed at Soesterberg. Note the unusually tall pylons on the drop tanks. (USAF)

ability of the F-86F at over 35,000 ft. This was further increased by eliminating the leading edge slats, thus smoothing the air flow over the entire wing. North American engineers designed an entire new wing leading edge that was extended 6 inches at the wing root, and 3 inches at the wing tip. Since this "6-3" extension was ahead of the wing spar, and movable parts were eliminated, the engineers designed an additional fuel tank into the leading edge extension, which added 130 gallons to the internal fuel capacity of the Sabre. A six inch

The first TF-86F on the ramp at Edwards AFB in 1953. The TF-86F had a six foot splice added into the fuselage to accommodate the second cockpit. In addition, the wings were moved aft 10 inches. This first TF-86F did not have the "6-3" wing. It was destroyed in a crash on March 17th 1954. (NAA)

An armorer loads .50 caliber ammunition into the forward ammo container on a 21st FBW F-86F at Chambley AB, France in 1955. A 750 lb. M117 General Purpose Bomb waits on the trailer to be loaded on the inboard pylon. The aircraft carries the three yellow and black bands to indicate the commander's Sabre of the 531st FBS. (NAA)

WARBIRDTECH
SERIES

high vertical "fence" was added at 70% of the wing span, to smooth the air flow over the ailerons.

The best part of this development was that the entire "6-3 extension" could be built as a "kit" and retrofitted to any late F-86E or F Sabre. The first fifty "kits" were rushed to Korea, where they were added to certain aircraft being flown by aggressive pilots, i.e., the hot MiG killers got the "kits." With the addition of the "6-3 hard wing," a Sabre pilot could now maneuver with the MiG at combat altitudes, thus eliminating one of the MiGs last advantages. The MiGs still had the altitude advantage, but that was all they retained of the advantages they enjoyed early in the war.

A USAF crew chief talks with the pilot of an F-86F from the 4521st CCTS, the last unit in the active Air Force to fly the F-86F. The final flight took place at Nellis AFB on June 27th 1966. The unit was training pilots to fly the F-86 under the Military Assistance Program. Note the updated "armament placard" and ejector seat triangle. (USAF)

The second TF-86F Transonic Trainer during takeoff of its first flight on August 5th 1954. The second TF-86F differed from the first in having the "6-3" wing with slats and wingtip extensions, and it was armed with a pair of .50 caliber machine guns. The taller tail and underside strake are clearly visible. (NAA)

The Paper Tiger, *an F-86F-10 assigned to Capt. Harold Fischer in the 39th FIS in early 1953. Capt. Fischer was a double ace with 10 victories before he was shot down. He marked his victories on the Sabre using small red MiG silhouettes. (via Larry Davis)*

The "6-3 hard wing" was added to production aircraft beginning with the 171st F-86F-25 and 200th F-30. Although very few F-25s went to Korea, the F-30s were heavily involved in the fighting, both with and without the "6-3 wing." The first F-30 fighter bombers went to the 18th Fighter Bomber Wing at Osan (K-55), where they replaced the very tired F-51D Mustangs that had been involved in the war almost from the first days. The 18th FBW began conversion into the F-86F-30 in January 1953. The 8th FBW at Suwon was the second fighter bomber unit to convert to F-86Fs, when they turned in their veteran Lockheed F-80Cs in April 1953. All these slat-winged F-30s were subsequently retrofitted with "6-3 hard wing kits" during the last half of 1953.

The personnel involved in supporting an F-86 mission in Korea included 1) the crew chief, 2) armorer 3) Ops Officer 4) Chaplain 5) radar technician 6) clerk 7) air police 8) radio technician 9) anti-aircraft gunner 10) firefighter 11) supply 12) gun camera technician 13) cook 14) refueling 15) refueling 16) medic 17) medic 18) firefighter 19) firefighter. These 19 people all helped put Lt. Robert Carter and his 4th FIG F-86F into the air in Korea. (USAF)

A crew chief from the 4th FIG checks the boresighting on The 6 Mes, *a 4th FIG F-86F at Kimpo in 1952. The guns and APG-30 radar were sighted in to converge at 750 yards, unless changed by the assigned pilot. (Larry Davis)*

There were two other variants of the F-86F that were built in significant numbers—the F-35 and F-40. The F-35 was the first Sabre variant capable of delivering a nuclear weapon. The F-35 was equipped with a Low Altitude Bombing System (LABS) computer, which allowed the Sabre to deliver the 1200 lb. "special store," a Mk 12 atomic bomb, by "tossing" the weapon at the target so that the Sabre could safely leave the area before the blast. North American/Inglewood built two hundred sixty five F-86F-35s, most of which were delivered to squadrons on duty with the US Air Forces / Europe.

The F-86F-40 was a further development of the "6-3" wing. The F-40 was specifically developed for use by the Japanese Air Self Defense Force, which was slated for Sabre equipment in 1956, and for manufacture by Mitsubishi Heavy Industries. Beginning in 1956, the USAF sent a number of veteran F-86Fs from units in Korea to the JASDF training units that were beginning conversion training with the Sabre. Since many of these JASDF pilots were World War Two veterans with no jet experience at all, the North American engineers, JASDF and USAF personnel involved in the conversion training, decided that a return to the slatted wings should be accomplished to make the conversion training as easy as possible for the fledgling JASDF pilot corps. North American's engineers had no problem re-installing the leading edge slats on

An element of 335th FIS F-86Fs patrol near the Yalu River searching for MiGs in the late Fall of 1952. As soon as the MiGs are sighted, both pilots will drop their underwing tanks. Both aircraft exhibit the late 1952 4th FIG markings of FEAF yellow and black ID bands on the fuselage and wings, with a similar yellow and black group marking on the tail. (Karl Dittmer)

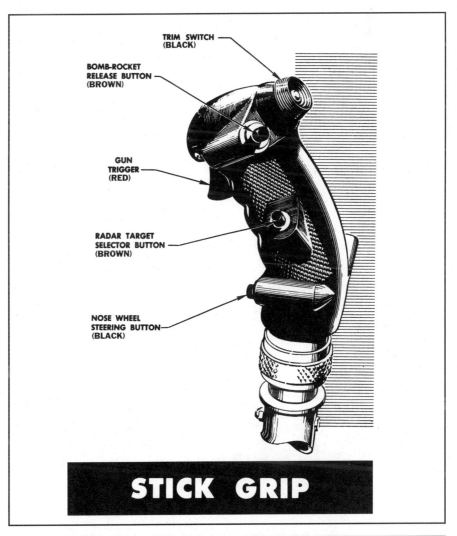

TRIM SWITCH
(BLACK)

BOMB-ROCKET
RELEASE BUTTON
(BROWN)

GUN
TRIGGER
(RED)

RADAR TARGET
SELECTOR BUTTON
(BROWN)

NOSE WHEEL
STEERING BUTTON
(BLACK)

STICK GRIP

MiG Mad Mavis *was the F-86F-5 assigned to Lt. Col. George Ruddell, CO of the 39th FIS and an eight victory ace in Korea. Lt. Col. Ruddell's F-5 has had one of the "6-3 wing kits" added, which effectively brought his airplane up to F-30 standard. The three yellow bands around the nose indicated that he was a squadron commander.* (Larry Davis)

the "6-3 wing." This increased the low speed control that had been lost through elimination of the slats on the Korean War MiG-hunters. In addition, a twelve inch extension was added to each wing tip for better high altitude maneuverability. North American/Inglewood built three hundred sets of air frame parts, which were then assembled by Mitsubishi. Two minor variants played very significant roles in

An F-86F-10 is about to be uncovered for the days mission. How cold did it get in Korea? How about -40°F on the Kimpo ramp! All the flying surfaces are covered and hot air will be pumped into the nose intake to warm all the engine fluids and electronics. (USAF)

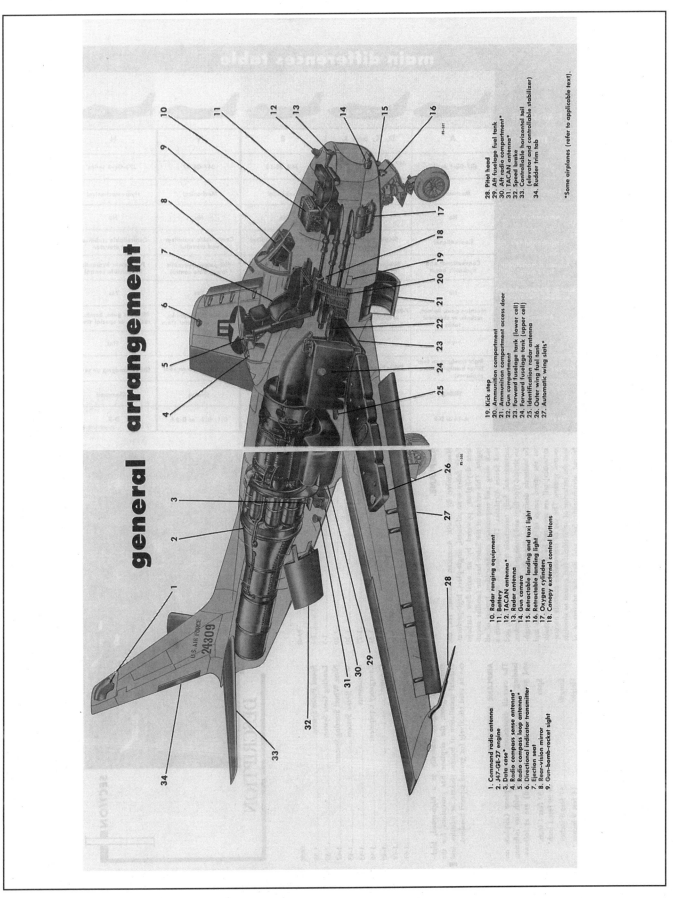

general arrangement

1. Command radio antenna
2. J47-GE-27 engine
3. Data case*
4. Radio compass sense antenna*
5. Radio compass loop antenna*
6. Directional indicator transmitter
7. Ejection seat
8. Rear-vision mirror
9. Gun-bomb-rocket sight
10. Radar ranging equipment
11. Battery
12. TACAN antenna*
13. Radar antenna
14. Gun camera
15. Retractable landing and taxi light
16. Retractable landing light
17. Oxygen cylinders
18. Canopy external control buttons
19. Kick step
20. Ammunition compartment
21. Ammunition compartment access door
22. Gun compartment
23. Forward fuselage tank (lower cell)
24. Forward fuselage tank (upper cell)
25. Identification radar antenna
26. Outer wing fuel tank
27. Automatic wing slots
28. Pitot head
29. Aft fuselage fuel tank
30. Aft radio compartment*
31. TACAN antenna*
32. Speed brake
33. Controllable horizontal tail (controllable and controllable stabilizer)
34. Rudder trim tab

*Some airplanes (refer to applicable text).

Schematic drawing cutaway of typical F-86 day fighter.

A flight of 39th FIS F-86Fs return from MiG Alley in the Spring of 1953. All four aircraft have had "6-3 wing kits" added. The third aircraft in line is Lt. James Thompson's famous The Huff *prior to his engagement with a MiG adorned with a green dragon. The formidable Korean landscape is shown to advantage. (Fred Chapman)*

future fighter evolution. They were known as GUNVAL and HAYMAKER.

GUNVAL

One of the biggest complaints of the pilots in Korea was a lack of hitting power against the MiGs. The MiG-15 was well armored in all the vital areas, and the six .50s weren't heavy enough to bring them down with regularity. It was not unusual for a Sabre pilot to empty his .50 calibre magazines (1600+ rounds) into a MiG, only to see the MiG flee smoking, back across the Yalu

Little Rita, *Lt. Dick Geiger's 16th FIS F-86F-5, has had the "6-3 wing kit" added. With the 6-3 wing, the juncture of the leading edge of the wing and the fuselage overlapped the gun bay door. North American solved this problem by making a small triangular piece removable. (Dick Geiger)*

A flight of early F-86Fs from the 51st FIG, bank away from the camera toward MiG Alley. The new "6-3 wing leading edge kit" is easily discerned on all four aircraft. North American initially sent fifty "6-3 kits" to Korea, which were promptly installed on aircraft assigned to "aggressive" pilots; i.e., the Big Hunters! (USAF)

WARBIRD**TECH**
S E R I E S

Project GUNVAL pilots climb into the cockpit of four of the 20mm cannon-armed F-86F-2s at Kimpo in 1953. Six GUNVAL aircraft were sent to Korea for combat testing. After problems with ingestion of gun gas from the 20MM cannons were solved, the modified Sabres performed quite well. The T-160 20MM cannon was then standardized as the M39, and installed in many new fighter types, including the F-86H, F-100, and F-101. (Paul Peterson)

to safety. Early in 1952, North American and Air Force, using the Ford-built T-160 20mm cannon, worked together to rectify the armament problem. North American Armament Chief Engineer Paul Peterson had the task of reworking the F-86F airframe to accept the T-160 cannons.

The project was known as GUNVAL. North American pulled four F-86Es (51-2803, -2819, -2826, and -2836) and six

335th FIS armorers work on the T-160 20mm cannons installed in Capt. Lonnie Moore's F-86F-2 GUNVAL aircraft at K-14 in 1953. Capt. Moore shot down 1½ MiGs with the GUNVAL F-2 before suffering a flameout in April 1953 and ejecting over the Yellow Sea. Note the painted on third gun port. (Paul Peterson)

A pair of 25th FIS F-86s taxi to the active runway at Suwon in the Spring of 1953. The near aircraft is an F-1 with a "6-3 kit" added, while the trailing airplane is This'll Kill Ya, the World Record holding F-86E. Mixed flights of F-86Es and Fs were normal through the end of the war. (Fred Chapman)

The Old Man *was Col. Walter Benz, CO of the 8th FBG at Suwon when the unit transitioned into F-86F-30 fighter bombers. His aircraft is shown with some of the many ordnance types that it could carry. Behind the 1800 rounds of .50 caliber ammunition are (from left) an M64 1000 lb. GP bomb, an M117 750 lb. GP bomb, and M43 500 lb. GP bomb; plus the underwing fuel tanks. (NAA)*

F-86F (51-2855, -2861, -2867, -2868, -2884, and -2900) from the Inglewood production line and installed four of the T-160 20mm cannons in place of the standard M3 machine gun armament. The T-160 20mm cannon was a gas-operated, belt-fed, electrically fired, percussion charged weapon, with a rate of fire of 1500 rounds/minute (The M3 fired 1100 rds./min.). The Ford-built T-160 was a much larger weapon than the M3, and required that the forward fuselage, gun bays, ammunition bays, and gun blast panel be redesigned. The forward fuselage was strengthened to absorb the increased shock of the cannons.

All the T-160 armed aircraft were designated as F-86F-2, whether they began as F-86Es or Fs. All were further modified with the "6-3 hard wing" as installed on the latest combat Sabres. The gun sight remained the type A-4 using the AN/APG-30 ranging radar in the nose. George Welch flew the initial

Armorers from No. 2 Squadron set the fuses on an M64 1000 lb. bomb that will be hung on aircraft "M," F-86F-30 #52-4344. No. 2 squadron was equipped with 22 brand new F-86F-30s. Note that the leading edge of a "short-chord" wing does not extend across the ammunition bay door. (SAAF)

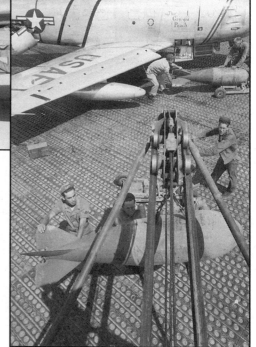

Armorers prepare to load a pair of M64 1000 lb. bombs under the wing of The Georgia Peach, *an F-86F-30 from the 36th FBS at K-13 in June 1953. Both the 8th and 18th FBGs received early F-86F-30, which had the reinforced fighter bomber wing having dual hard points, but having the non-6-3 wing with leading edge slats. (USAF)*

WARBIRDTECH
S E R I E S

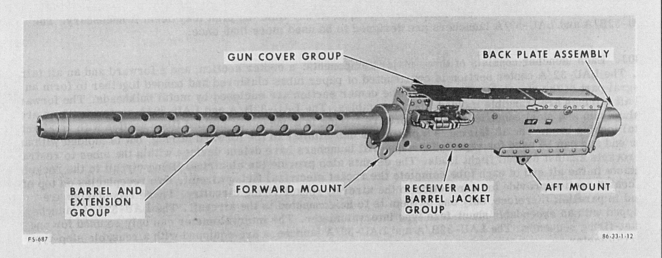

Figure 1-12.   M-3 Gun

1-31.   GUN, M-3, .50-CALIBER (F-86F AIRCRAFT).

1-32.   The F-86F aircraft gunnery system consists of six Type M-3 .50-caliber machine guns and related equipment.   Three guns are installed in each right and left gun bay compartment adjacent to the cockpit. Ammunition and expanded case and link compartments are directly below the gun bay compartments.

1-33.   The M-3 gun is an automatic recoil-operated, link-belt fed, air-cooled weapon.   (See figure 1-12.) The gun has a firing rate of 1,150 to 1,250 rounds of .50-caliber ammuntion per minute.   A metallic link belt of the disintegrating type is used to feed the ammuntion into the gun.   As the gun bolt mechanism is oper- ated, the belt moves into the gun.   The round is removed from the belt and the link is ejected into the expended link compartment.   After a round is fired, the empty case is ejected into the expended case com- partment.   The gun bolt mechanism is operated by recoil forces from the explosive gases of the cartridges.

1-34.   PHYSICAL CHARACTERISTICS.

1-35.   Weight:

  a.   Weight of gun assembled: approximately 69 pounds.

1-36.   Dimensions:

  a.   Length of gun assembled: 57. 5 inches.

  b.   Width of gun assembled: approximately 5 inches.

  c.   Height of gun assembled: approximately 9 inches.

Type M-3 .50 calibre machine gun and characteristics as found on F-86A, E, or F.

firing tests in -2803 near Catalina Island. The weapons operated per- fectly. All tests were flown below 35,000 feet. After satisfactory com- pletion of the firing tests, Lt. Col. Clayton Peterson, GUNVAL project officer, took eight of the F-2s to Korea aboard the USS Windham Bay for combat trials against the MiGs.

All the GUNVAL aircraft were assigned to the 335th FIS/4th FIW at Kimpo, although only six aircraft were ever actually in Korea at any one time. The F-2s were all marked the same as any standard F-86F, with black and yellow FEAF ID bands on the wings and fuselage, plus the yellow and black tail stripe indicating an aircraft from the 4th

FIW. In addition, there was a "third gun port" painted on the nose under the two 20mm muzzles to make the F-2s appear to be the same as other Sabres in the theater—at least at first glance.

Colonel Peterson and his team went to Kimpo in January 1953, beginning the combat trials almost immediately. The GUNVAL aircraft suffered a variety of problems, including flameouts at combat altitude whenever all four cannons were fired. It was discovered that gun gas from the 20mm cannons was being ingested into the intake causing a compressor stall. It never happened during the tests in California because the tests were flown at lower altitudes than where combat was taking place, i.e., at 40,000 feet+. However, the results of the combat tests were favorable. Using only two guns at a time, the GUNVAL Sabres fired almost 109,000 rounds. They encountered MiGs on forty one missions, with

Head-on view of an F-86F-30 at Osan-ni in the summer of 1953 showing the placement of the wing hard points, which carried the fuel tanks and ordnance. This aircraft has had the "6-3 wing kit" installed. The small size of the APG-30 radar radome can be seen. (James Sullivan)

WARBIRD**TECH**
S E R I E S

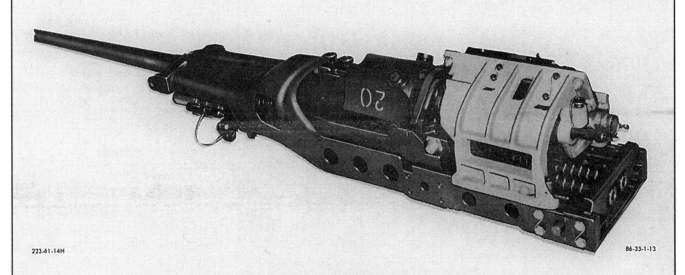

223-61-14H
86-33-1-13

Figure 1-13. M-39 Gun

1-37. GUN, M-39A2, 20-MILLIMETER (F-86H AIRCRAFT).

1-38. F-86H aircraft AF52-2090 and all later aircraft are equipped with four M-39A2 20-millimeter guns and related equipment. The equipment includes provisions for purging gun, ammunition, and expended-link compartments of potentially dangerous accumulations of explosive gun gases during and after gunfire. Two guns are on each side of the aircraft in the gun bay compartments below the cockpit. Two ammunition containers (cans) are directly below each gun bay compartment, and the expended links are retained in a compartment between the ammunition containers. Expended cases are ejected overboard.

1-39. The M-39A2 gun is a 20-millimeter, gas-operated, belt-fed, electrically fired, revolver-type weapon. (See figure 1-13.) Each gun is capable of rapid fire of from 1,500 to 1,700 rounds of ammunition per minute, with an effective range of 3,500 feet. The gun may be fed from either the left or right side. A metallic link belt of the disintegrating type is used to feed the ammunition into the gun. The main components of the gun consist of a barrel assembly, a receiver assembly, a drum and cradle assembly, a feeder assembly, and a gun charger assembly. The main components are assembled together, dependent upon whether the gun is to be used for a left or right installation.

1-40. PHYSICAL CHARACTERISTICS.

1-41. Weight:

a. Weight of assembled gun: 179 pounds.

1-42. Dimensions:

a. Length of assembled gun: 72.4 inches.

b. Width of assembled gun: approximately 12 inches.

c. Height of assembled gun: approximately 12 inches.

1-43 through 1-53.   (Deleted)

(All data deleted from page 1-14, and pages
1-15, 1-16, figure 1-14 deleted)

M-39A2 (T-160) 20mm cannon and characteristics as found on GUNVAL F-86F-2s and F-86H-5.

Hallie's Comet IV, *the F-86F flown by Maj. William Rice, commanding the 335th Fighter Day Squadron at Chitose AB, Japan in 1956. Chitose AB was "home plate" for the 4th FDW prior to re-deployment back to the US after their "short TDY" of seven years! Note the addition of an anti-glare panel and "US AIR FORCE" logo to the fuselage. (via Mike Fox)*

these results; six MiGs destroyed, three probably destroyed, and thirteen damaged.

Had the GUNVAL pilots been able to fire all four cannons at the same time, the results would have been better. Mr. Paul Peterson, the North American Armament Chief that accompanied the project to Korea, came up with a simple "fix" that cured the compressor stall problem. A simple horseshoe clip installed in the blast tube of the cannon broke up the gun gas before it could enter the intake. Two GUNVAL aircraft were lost because of the compressor stall problem, including one flown by Capt. Lonnie Moore, the ace from the 335th FIS. Although the GUN-VAL combat test verified the T-160

installation in an F-86, the installation would not become a production item until well into the F-86H program. It was to be the main armament of the F-100 Super Sabre and F-101 Voodoo.

HAYMAKER

Following on the heels of the successful ASHTRAY RF-86A modification, North American began a program to factory-build the reconnaissance Sabre using an F-86F-30 airframe. The initial HAYMAKER RF-86Fs, built at the TSUIKI REMCO facility, were virtually identical to the ASHTRAY RF-86As, with a pair of K-9 and a single K-25 cameras mounted in the forward fuselage. Ballast was added to the nose to

keep the center of gravity as it was on a gun-equipped F-86F. These aircraft were rushed to Korea in the Spring of 1953 and assigned to the 15th TRS/67th TRW at Kimpo, alongside the RF-86As. In the early Summer of 1953, the first true factory-built RF-86Fs went to Kimpo. The factory-designed RF-86Fs differed from both the ASHTRAY and HAYMAKER aircraft in having a pair of K-22 and a single K-17 camera installed. The K-22s, having a much longer focal length than the older K-9s, necessitated bulging the gun bay doors for installation. North American built several RF-86Fs for the US Air Force, but the type was never standardized, being replaced by RF-84F Thunderflash reconnaissance fighters. However, both the Japanese Air Self Defense Force and the Republic of Korea Air Force had several squadrons equipped with both North American and Mitsubishi-built RF-86F aircraft.

One of the few Air National Guard units to fly the F-86F was Colorado's 120th FIS. And not just any F-86Fs either. The MINUTE MEN aerobatic team flew F-86F-2s, the Sabres involved in the Project GUNVAL 20MM cannon combat tests. Note only two gun ports on each aircraft. The second aircraft flies the Slot position, with his tail directly in the exhaust of the Leader. The F-2s had "6-3" wings with slats and extended wingtips installed prior to transfer to the 120th FIS.
(Bob Esposito)

WARBIRDTECH
SERIES

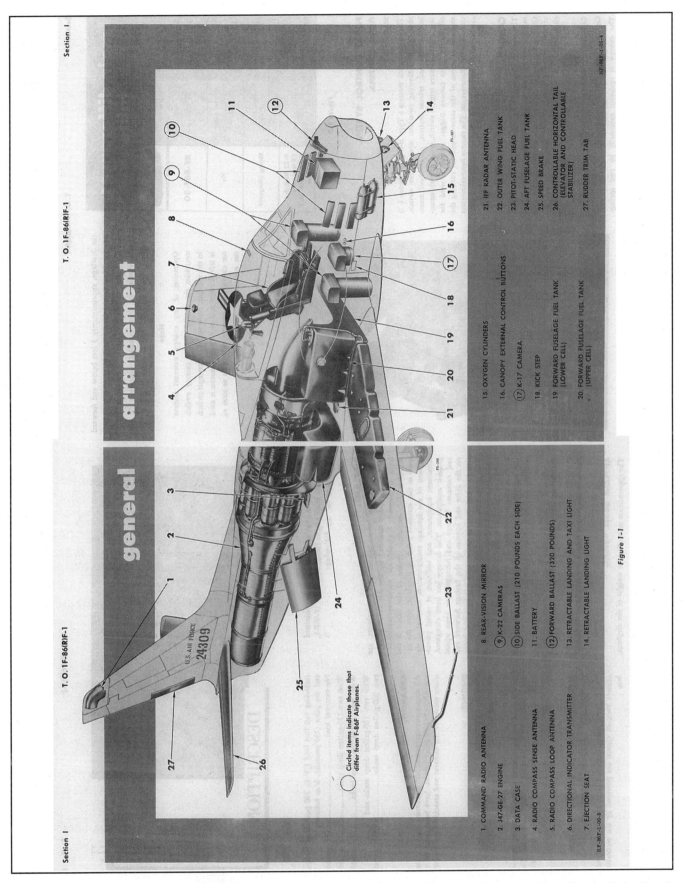

general arrangement

1. COMMAND RADIO ANTENNA
2. J47-GE-27 ENGINE
3. DATA CASE
4. RADIO COMPASS SENSE ANTENNA
5. RADIO COMPASS LOOP ANTENNA
6. DIRECTIONAL INDICATOR TRANSMITTER
7. EJECTION SEAT
8. REAR-VISION MIRROR
9. K-22 CAMERAS
10. SIDE BALLAST (210 POUNDS EACH SIDE)
11. BATTERY
12. FORWARD BALLAST (320 POUNDS)
13. RETRACTABLE LANDING AND TAXI LIGHT
14. RETRACTABLE LANDING LIGHT

15. OXYGEN CYLINDERS
16. CANOPY EXTERNAL CONTROL BUTTONS
17. K-17 CAMERA
18. KICK STEP
19. FORWARD FUSELAGE FUEL TANK (LOWER CELL)
20. FORWARD FUSELAGE FUEL TANK (UPPER CELL)
21. IFF RADAR ANTENNA
22. OUTER WING FUEL TANK
23. PITOT-STATIC HEAD
24. AFT FUSELAGE FUEL TANK
25. SPEED BRAKE
26. CONTROLLABLE HORIZONTAL TAIL (ELEVATOR AND CONTROLLABLE STABILIZER)
27. RUDDER TRIM TAB

Circled items indicate those that differ from F-86F Airplanes.

Figure 1-1

Schematic drawing of RF-86F showing various cameras and equipment found only on the RF-86F as built by North American Aviation.

F-86H: LAST OF THE SPORTS JOBS

THE FIGHTER-BOMBER SABRE

The F-86H was intended to be the ultimate Sabre design, the one that could do it all—fight the MiGs, drop bombs, shoot missiles, even deliver nuclear weapons. And do it better than any comparable aircraft in the world. And in many ways, the F-86H lived up to the design expectations. It was the fastest, highest flying, longest ranged, most heavily armed Sabre ever built. The trouble was that there were already designs ready to fly that obsoleted the F-86H even before it made its maiden flight—including a design for something called the SUPER SABRE!

During the early stages of the war in Korea, Air Force knew that it needed a true jet fighter bomber, something akin to the World War Two Republic P-47 Thunderbolt, but having a jet engine. They had a World War Two jet fighter that

George "Wheaties" Welch stands ready to board the first YF-86H, #52-1975 for the first flight on April 30th 1953. The larger intake opening is apparent, as is the clamshell opening canopy. The instrument probe in the radome, and the pitot heads under the fuselage, were not found on production aircraft. Note the dual front nose wheel doors. (NAA)

The YF-86H shares the ramp with other test aircraft at Edwards AFB, California including the first F-86F-5 and the second F-86D-1 in Spring 1953. Two YF-86Hs were built at North American's factory in Inglewood, California. But all production aircraft were built in Columbus, Ohio. (Al Schmidt)

WARBIRD**TECH**
S E R I E S

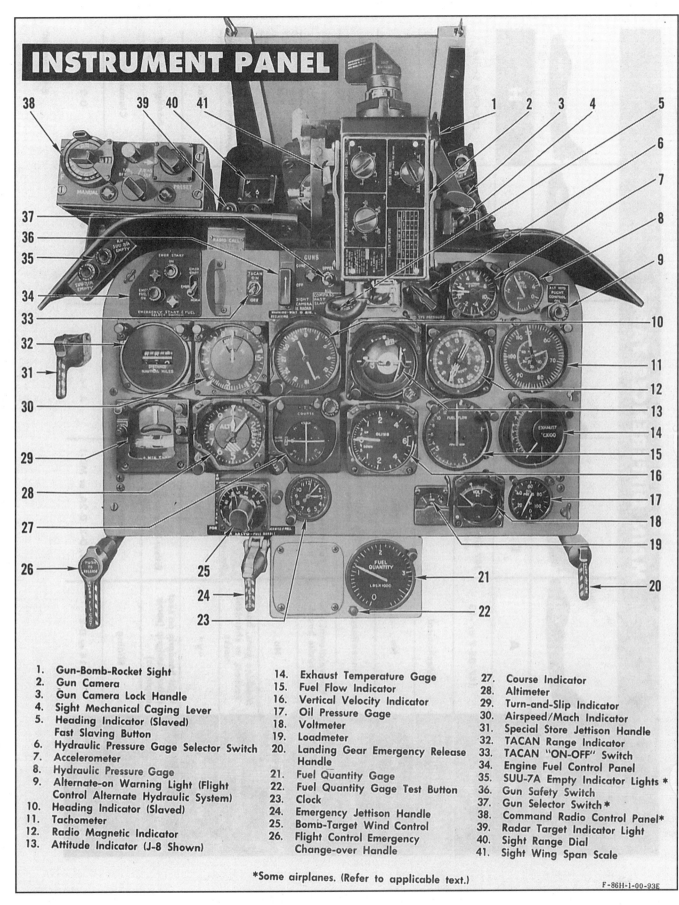

INSTRUMENT PANEL

1. Gun-Bomb-Rocket Sight
2. Gun Camera
3. Gun Camera Lock Handle
4. Sight Mechanical Caging Lever
5. Heading Indicator (Slaved)
   Fast Slaving Button
6. Hydraulic Pressure Gage Selector Switch
7. Accelerometer
8. Hydraulic Pressure Gage
9. Alternate-on Warning Light (Flight
   Control Alternate Hydraulic System)
10. Heading Indicator (Slaved)
11. Tachometer
12. Radio Magnetic Indicator
13. Attitude Indicator (J-8 Shown)
14. Exhaust Temperature Gage
15. Fuel Flow Indicator
16. Vertical Velocity Indicator
17. Oil Pressure Gage
18. Voltmeter
19. Loadmeter
20. Landing Gear Emergency Release
    Handle
21. Fuel Quantity Gage
22. Fuel Quantity Gage Test Button
23. Clock
24. Emergency Jettison Handle
25. Bomb-Target Wind Control
26. Flight Control Emergency
    Change-over Handle
27. Course Indicator
28. Altimeter
29. Turn-and-Slip Indicator
30. Airspeed/Mach Indicator
31. Special Store Jettison Handle
32. TACAN Range Indicator
33. TACAN "ON-OFF" Switch
34. Engine Fuel Control Panel
35. SUU-7A Empty Indicator Lights *
36. Gun Safety Switch
37. Gun Selector Switch *
38. Command Radio Control Panel*
39. Radar Target Indicator Light
40. Sight Range Dial
41. Sight Wing Span Scale

*Some airplanes. (Refer to applicable text.)

F-86H-1-00-93E

Cockpit layout for the F-86H.

Crew chief's and armorers ready an F-86H-10 assigned to the 83rd FDW at Seymour Johnson AFB, North Carolina for another flight. The H-10 was the last day fighter variant of the F-86 to come from the North American assembly lines. (David Menard)

was performing the role of fighter bomber in the Lockheed F-80C Shooting Star. They also had a long range escort fighter doing the same type of mission, the Republic F-84 Thunderjet. And of course, they were still using the renowned F-51D Mustangs as close support

aircraft. But all three types lacked the ability to effectively mix it up with the Russian MiGs. Only the F-86 could handle the MiGs, and the Sabre had a very limited fighter bomber capability.

North American Aviation and the Air Force did succeed in developing the basic F-86 design into an aircraft with fighter bomber capabilities in the F-86F series. But loading up the J47 powered F-86F with a couple of 1,000 lb. bombs, up to sixteen 5 inch HVAR rockets, or a single 1200 lb. "special store," cost the F-86F in speed and range, both of which were certainly a bad compromise at the very least. What was needed was an F-86 designed from the outset as a fighter bomber, but at the speed and range equal to or better than the day fighter types. On March 16th 1951, North American was authorized to begin design and construction on just such a Sabre. One year later, they had the idea down on paper and metal was being cut on the NA-187.

The new aircraft was designed from the outset to be

A pair of 474th FBW F-86H-5s on the ramp at Clovis AFB, New Mexico in 1956. The H-5 was the first of the H models to be armed with the M39 20мм cannons, having a cyclic rate of 1500 rounds per minute. The large faded dayglo number "3" on the fuselage was left over from a gunnery competition at Nellis AFB. (Robb Satterfield)

COCKPIT . . . LEFT SIDE

1. Anti-G Suit Pressure-regulating Valve
2. Circuit-breaker Panel
3. Thunderstorm Light
4. Circuit-breaker Panel
5. Wing Flap Handle
6. Canopy and Windshield Defrost Handles
7. Left Forward Switch Panel
8. Air Conditioning Control Panel
9. Engine Control Panel
10. Take-off Trim Indicator Light
11. Throttle Friction Wheel
12. Rudder Trim Switch
13. Flight Control Switch
14. Throttle
15. Radar Range Sweep Rheostat
16. UHF Command Radio Control Panel (Panel shown for unmodified airplanes)
17. Armament Control Panel
18. Sight Function Selector Unit
19. Ground Fire Safety Switch*
20. Rocket Projector Release
21. Strike Camera Timer
22. Speed Brake Dump Valve Lever*

*Some airplanes. (Refer to applicable text.)

86H-1-00-78F

FS-317

COCKPIT . . . RIGHT SIDE

1. Fire-warning Panel
2. Spare Lamps
3. Cabin Pressure Altimeter
4. Deleted
5. Lighting Control Panel
6. Circuit-breaker Panel
7. Thunderstorm Light
8. Map Case
9. Sight Ground Test Plug
10. Circuit-breaker Panel
11. Cockpit Utility Light
12. SIF Control Panel
13. Canopy Initiator Lever Guard
14. IFF Control Panel
15. Oxygen Regulator
16. Right Forward Switch Panel

FS-316

F-86H-1-00-79D

Left and right views of the cockpit layout for the F-86H.

An F-86H-5 undergoes a full maintenance check of the engine, weapons, and cockpit, on the open ramp at Clovis AFB, NM, now Cannon AFB. The F-86H was the first true fighter bomber variant of the Sabre. (NAA)

powered by an entirely new powerplant, the GE J73 with almost twice the thrust of the J47—over 8900 lbs. of thrust without using an afterburner. The J73 engine, being both physically larger and requiring a much greater volume of air, meant that the basic F-86 fuselage dimensions would have to be enlarged. The fuselage was first deepened six inches throughout its length. This would allow the air intake tube size to be increased to give the J73 the required amount of air. The removable aft fuselage section was lengthened 14 inches in the tailpipe area to cover the increased length of the J73.

The canopy developed for the F-86D, with its distinctive clamshell opening, replaced the typical Sabre sliding canopy, was added to the re-designed forward fuselage. A larger vertical fin assembly was used, but with a smaller rudder than found on the F-86F. Initially the wing design from the early F-86F-25/-30 series was chosen. It had the narrow chord and short wing span

The 474th FBW took their F-86Hs to Narsarssuak AB, Greenland in Fall 1956 in a deployment during the Suez Crisis. Note the wooden ladder used to enter the cockpit, which was a hold-over from the F-84 era. (USAF)

The ramp at Clovis AFB, New Mexico with two F-86H wings being seen. The aircraft with the striped tails are from the 474th FBW, while the solid color tails with lightning bolts belong to the 312th FBW. The Air Force only had six F-86H wings, as the H was quickly supplanted by the F-100. (NAA)

Red 4, an F-86H-10 from the 474th FBW, leaves the runway at Clovis AFB in 1956. Note that while the engine is running, hydraulic pressure keeps the main landing gear doors closed, as well as the rear portion of the nose door assembly. (NAA)

with slats, but with the fighter bomber strength and underwing hard points. The stabilizer used on the NA-187 was the single slab type developed for the F-86D, with irreversible flight controls.

Initially, the NA-187 was to have the standard F-86 armament of six M3 .50 caliber machine guns. But before the first aircraft was finished, Air Force called for a change in the armament. Combat in Korea had clearly shown that the six .50s weren't heavy enough to bring down the MiGs. Ford Motor Company, working with North American and Air Force, had developed the T-160 20mm cannon for use in future fighter designs. Project GUNVAL was the successful combat test of the T-160 cannon mounted in several F-86F air frames in Korea (see F-86F Project GUNVAL). The T-160 would be the primary armament of the NA-187, now designated F-86H by Air Force. However, none of these weapons would be avail-

This F-86H-5 is assigned to the 34th FDS, as part of the 413th Fighter Day Wing at George AFB, California. The 413th FDW was commanded by the colorful George Laven, and had some of the most colorful markings ever seen on F-86s, including the red and white checks on 34th vertical and horizontal surfaces. The H had a much smaller entry door than previous Sabre variants. (NAA)

An element of 10th FBS F-86H-10s over Germany in 1955, carrying 200 gallon underwing fuel tanks. The 50th FBW was based at Toul-Rosieres France and had a nuclear mission, which the F-86H could fly using the Low Altitude Bombing System, or LABS, which "tossed" the weapon onto the target. (David Menard)

The crew chief sits in the cockpit of an F-86H at Toul-Rosieres AB, France in 1956. All the landing gear bay doors have bled down to an open position after engine shutdown. (David Menard)

able for initial production of the H.

North American and Air Force concurred that production of the F-86H should begin using standard M3 .50 caliber guns. The initial contract called for two prototypes to be built by North American/Los Angeles, although all production aircraft were to be built at the North American plant in Columbus, Ohio. The armament problem had no impact on production of the prototypes, since neither was slated for armament anyway. In March

An F-86H from the 413th FDW, shares the ramp with an 8th FBW F-86F, as it has its guns bore sighted and test fired at Nellis AFB in 1956. The M39 cannons had a cyclic rate of 1500 rounds per minute, compared with the 1100 rounds/minute in the M3 .50 caliber machine gun equipped F-86F. (NAA)

WARBIRDTECH
SERIES

As the F-100 was phased into service, the F-86H was phased into the Air National Guard, where it served with distinction into the 1970s. This F-86H was the aircraft flown by the 101st TFS CO, as denoted by the 4 red stripes around the fuselage. The extended "6-3" wing with slats is clearly shown. (P.M. Paulsen)

1953, the first YF-86H, #52-1975, came off the assembly line at Inglewood. It looked like a Sabre—a fat Sabre! The wing span was the same at 37.12 feet. The fuselage length was 38.84 feet, up from 37.54 feet in the F-86F; and the height was set at 14.99 feet, a 3 inch increase over the F model. But that was where the similarities ended.

The empty weight jumped from 11,038 lbs. of the F-86F-30, to 14,218 lbs. in the YF-86H. The maximum takeoff weight leaped from 16,438 lbs. in the F, to 23,792 lbs. in the H. But even with the weight increase, the top speed increased to over 707 MPH. The service ceiling went to 51,500 feet, 3,000 feet higher than the F. Using the J73 engine meant that the rate of climb was almost 3000 feet/minute greater than the F—12,160 ft./min. And these performance figures were with a standard combat load-

ing. The internal fuel tankage was increased from 435 gallons to 570 gallons, resulting in an increase in the range of over 100 miles. With underwing drop tanks, the YF-86H had a range of 1360 miles.

Both the first and second prototypes (52-1975 and -1976) were powered by General Electric YJ-73-GE-3 engines rated at 8920 lbs. of thrust. A third prototype was also built at Inglewood as a static test aircraft. Since it was designed to be tested to destruction, the third prototype had no serial number. On May 9th

1953, following extensive taxi and brake tests, plus the usual amount of new airplane problems and sub-

TYPICAL EACH SIDE

BEWARE OF BLAST

DUST COVER ATTACH

F-86H-2-31-43

Figure 1-22. Vortex Generators

Vortex generators were added to the rear fuselage and horizontal tail surfaces to eliminate tail "shake."

Playboy *was an F-86H-5 assigned to the 104th TFS/Maryland ANG at Martin Field in 1957 The 104th converted from F-86Es to F-86Hs in December 1957. Except for gun blast panels and engine exhaust areas, the aircraft has been painted silver.* (Joe Bruch)

sequent repairs, North American test pilot Joe Lynch took the first YF-86H into the air for the first time. Both Lynch and Air Force were extremely happy with what they had.

In October 1951, even before the YF-86H was drawn on paper, Air Force ordered one hundred fifty production F-86Hs from North American. On November 3rd, 1952, after production of the prototype was underway, the order was increased to one hundred seventy-five aircraft. Several changes were ordered even before the YF-86H was rolled out. In October 1952 the "6-3 hard wing" was approved for production on the F-86F. Air Force also had North American incorporate the "6-3 wing" for production

on the F-86H, beginning with the 15th F-86H-1. Finally, in December 1952, the T-160 20mm cannon armament was ordered into production on the F-86H. However, the T-160 (designated M39 by the Air Force) would still not be available until production of the H was well underway. North American would build one hundred fifteen YF and F-86H-1s with M3 .50 caliber guns before the M39s were available.

The first production F-86H-1 came off the Columbus assembly line in August 1953, making its first flight from the Columbus Airport on September 4th. Most of the production aircraft were identical to the YF-86Hs with the exception of the wing design and the power-plant. The first fourteen H-1s still had the short span (37.12') wing, and they had a single point refueling system installed. Beginning with the fifteenth H-1 (52-1992), the production aircraft had the "6-3 hard wing" without leading edge slats. The wing was also extended in span twelve inches. The first sixty H-1s were powered by the J73-GE-3 engine rated at 8920 lbs. of thrust. However, the remainder of the pro-

Another silver-painted F-86H from the 104th TFS / Maryland ANG at Glenn L. Martin Field, has a tow target reel on the inboard pylon of the left wing. By the early 1960s, most Air Guard aircraft had the ANG badge on the tail, but had the US Air Force and USAF logos on the fuselage and wings. (Jim Sullivan)

WARBIRDTECH
SERIES

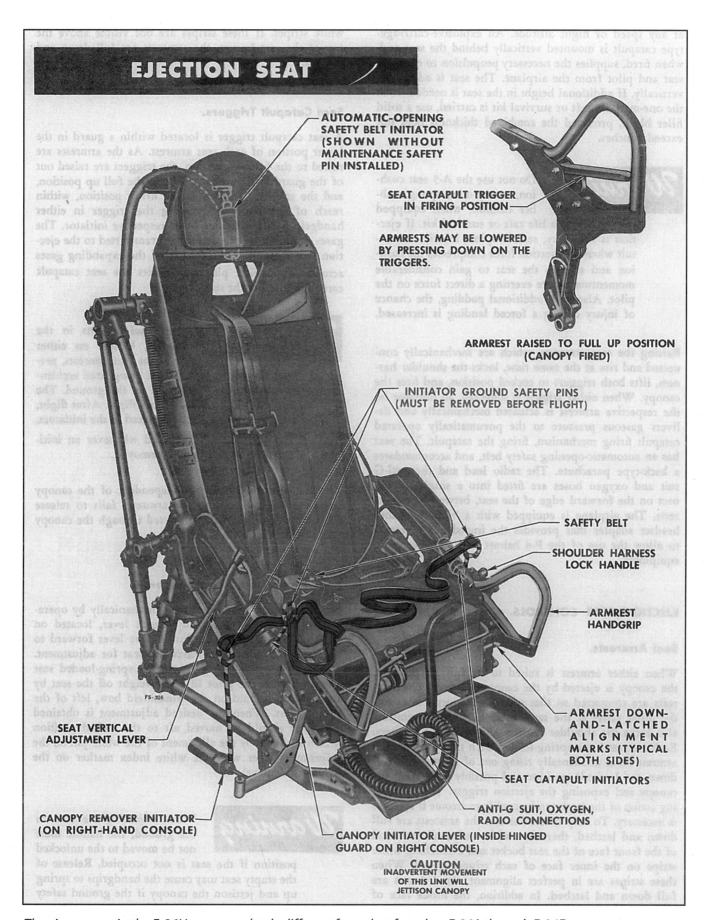

EJECTION SEAT

AUTOMATIC-OPENING
SAFETY BELT INITIATOR
(SHOWN WITHOUT
MAINTENANCE SAFETY
PIN INSTALLED)

SEAT CATAPULT TRIGGER
IN FIRING POSITION

NOTE
ARMRESTS MAY BE LOWERED
BY PRESSING DOWN ON THE
TRIGGERS.

ARMREST RAISED TO FULL UP POSITION
(CANOPY FIRED)

INITIATOR GROUND SAFETY PINS
(MUST BE REMOVED BEFORE FLIGHT)

SAFETY BELT

SHOULDER HARNESS
LOCK HANDLE

ARMREST
HANDGRIP

ARMREST DOWN-
AND-LATCHED
ALIGNMENT
MARKS (TYPICAL
BOTH SIDES)

SEAT CATAPULT INITIATORS

SEAT VERTICAL
ADJUSTMENT LEVER

ANTI-G SUIT, OXYGEN,
RADIO CONNECTIONS

CANOPY REMOVER INITIATOR
(ON RIGHT-HAND CONSOLE)

CANOPY INITIATOR LEVER (INSIDE HINGED
GUARD ON RIGHT CONSOLE)

CAUTION
INADVERTENT MOVEMENT
OF THIS LINK WILL
JETTISON CANOPY

FS-326

The ejector seat in the F-86H was completely different from that found on F-86A through F-86F.

A flight of four F-86Hs assigned to the 195th FIS/California ANG in the late 1950s. Most historians do not recognize the fact the 195th was equipped with F-86Hs, but photos do not lie. The aircraft are H-10s, with the extended "6-3" wing. (NAA)

duction of the F-86H was powered by the J73-GE-3A engine, rated at 9247 lbs of thrust. All F-86H-1s had the six M3 .50 caliber machine gun armament. North American / Columbus built one hundred seventy-three F-86H-1s (52-1977/-2089).

The F-86H-5 was the next variant from the Columbus assembly line. It was identical to the late H-1s with the J-73-GE-3A powerplant, but had the four M39 20mm cannons for the main armament. The M39 20mm cannon was a belt-fed weapon with an extremely high rate of fire—1500 rounds per minute, which was greater than that of the M3 .50 caliber gun. Each ammunition drum held a total of 150 rounds for a total of 600 rounds—about six seconds worth! Columbus built sixty H-5s in two batches, serials 52-2090/-2124 and 52-5729/-5753. The F-86H-10 was similar to the H-5 with some internal electrical and instrumentation modifications. The H-10 was the most numerous of the type as Columbus built three hundred H-10s (53-1229/-1528). The last ten H-

The 167th TFS/West Virginia ANG was the first Guard unit to convert to F-86Hs, in December 1957. All their aircraft were F-86H-1s, which still had the main armament of six .50 caliber machine guns. (Ron Picciani)

An F-86H from the 104th TFS/Maryland ANG on the ramp at NAS Lakehurst, New Jersey during the Pueblo Crisis of 1968. The aircraft is still in overall silver and carries the US Air Force logo and Tactical Air Command badge on the tail. The "0" in front of the serial number indicates the aircraft has been in service for over 10 years. (Bob Esposito)

WARBIRD**TECH**
SERIES

Index No.	Nomenclature	Figure No.
1	Armament	236
2	6 Fixed .50 Caliber Guns Equipment	236
3	Open Port Blast Panel	237
4	Low Altitude Bomb Gyro	234
5	A4 Gun Bomb Rocket Sight Installation	234
6	A4 Gunsight Computer Equipment	235
7	A4 Gunsight System Equipment 232,233
8	A4 Sighthead N9 Camera	242
9	Pneumatic Gun Charger Equipment	239
10	Impact Camera	337
11	Rocket Equipment	335
12	Rocket Mounts	336
13	Bomb Rack	326

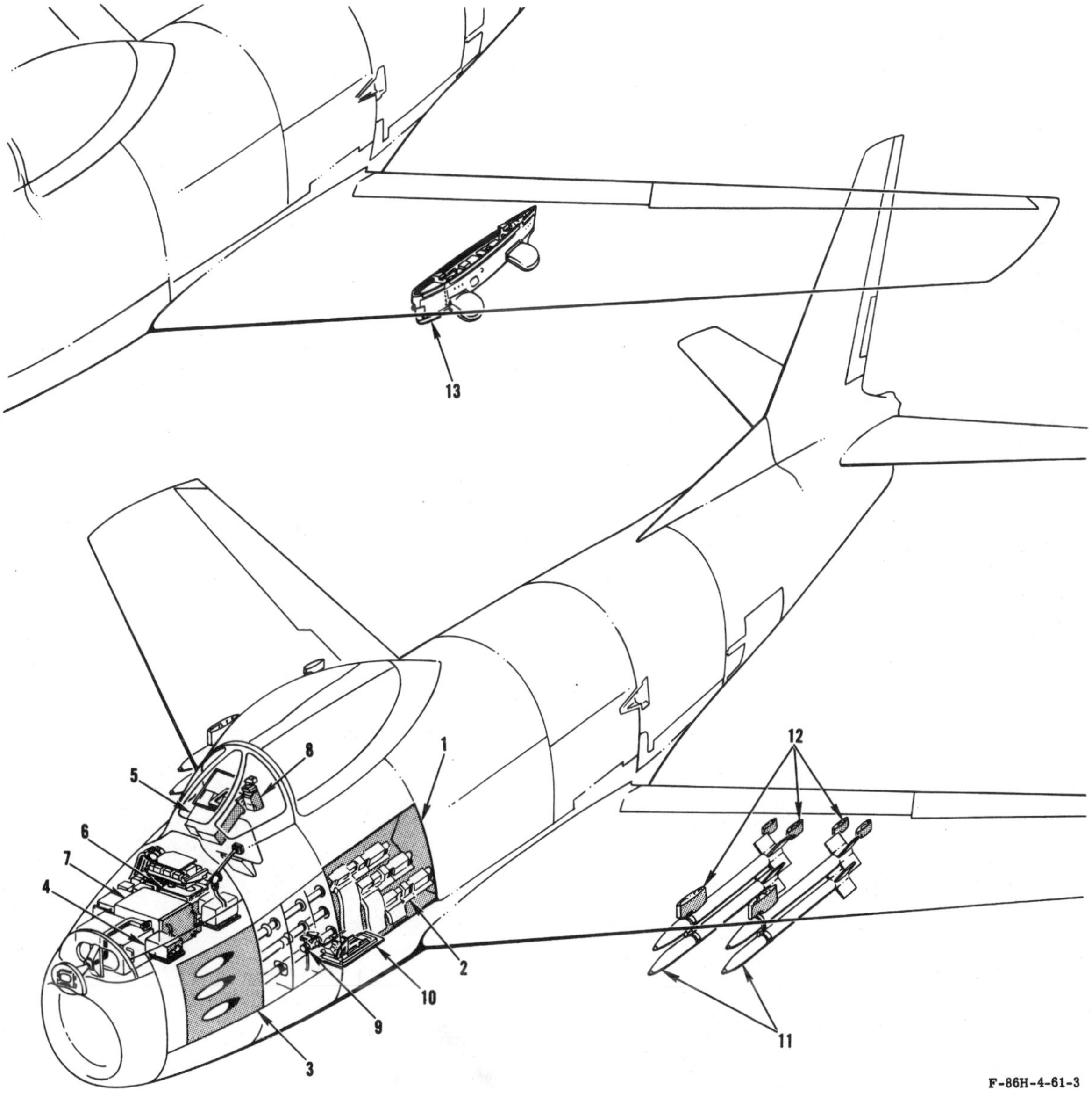

FIGURE 346 - ARMAMENT SYSTEM INSTALLATION

F-86H-4-61-3

Armament system components of the M-3 .50 caliber machine installation in F-86H-1s

An F-86H from the 104th TFS/Maryland ANG with AIM-9 Sidewinder missile launchers, sits on the ramp at Glenn L. Martin Field in 1970. The 104th TFS Hs were camouflaged in SEA tan and two greens, the standard tactical camouflage color used by the US Air Force during the war in Vietnam. Its pristine condition indicates the aircraft has just come from the paint shop. (Denis Hughes)

10s were delivered in March 1956. The wing design had changed once again as these last ten H-10s were delivered with leading edge slats on the "6-3 wing."

The F-86Hs began equipping active US Air Force units during the Fall of 1954 when the 312th Fighter Bomber Wing at Clovis AFB, NM converted from F-86Fs. Eventually six Air Force wings were equipped with F-86Hs—the 4th FDW, 50th FBW, 83rd FDW, 312th FBW, 413th FBW, and 474th FBW. Although the F-86H was the best of the basic Sabre designs, its demise as a front line aircraft was assured when the first F-100 Super Sabre broke the sonic barrier in level flight. By the end of 1957 only the 4th FDW at Seymour Johnson AFB, recently returned from a "short TDY" stint in Korea, was equipped with F-86Hs. And the 4th would finish converting to F-100Cs in the summer of 1958.

However, the F-86H had a long and storied career in the Air National Guard. Beginning with the first ANG squadron that converted to Hs in 1957, the "Last Of The Sport Jobs" would serve into the early 1970s. The 138th TFS/New York ANG, "The Boys From Syracuse," was the last F-86H squadron, converting to A-37Bs in the Fall of 1970.

Although never committed to actual combat, the F-86Hs were placed in harm's way. Two F-86H squadrons from the Massachusetts ANG, and one New York ANG F-86H squadron deployed to Phalsbourg AB, France during the October 1961 Berlin Crisis, where they remained for a year. Although capable of nuclear strikes, the ANG Hs were tasked with conventional fighter bomber missions only. It was during this crisis that the ANG F-86H inventory peaked at one hundred sixty-eight aircraft.

During the Pueblo Crisis of May 1968, the remaining two F-86H squadrons in the New York and Maryland Air Guard, were activated and deployed to Cannon AFB, NM for six months. Following phaseout from all active service with US Air Force and Air National Guard squadrons, a great many F-86Hs continued to fly "combat" as US Navy TOP GUN "aggressor" aircraft. Many an F-14 Tomcat driver found himself in the unenviable position of having an F-86H at his "6." And many more Navy pilots lined up to fly "The Last of the Sport Jobs!"

Both the 104th TFS/Maryland ANG, and the 138th TFS/New York ANG were activated once again during the Pueblo Crisis of May 1968. Both squadrons went to Cannon AFB, New Mexico, but only the Maryland unit took their airplanes and had tail codes, "CT" for Cannon AFB, applied. These Hs were some of the last Sabres to serve, being phased out of ANG service in the Fall of 1970. (Merle Olmsted)

NOTE Airplane principal dimensions are taken with the landing gear struts and tires inflated to the correct pressures. Other general data on the airplane is as follows:

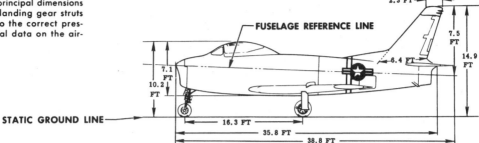

WING
Type . . . . Low
Airfoil Section
Root . . . . NACA 0012-64
Tip . . . . NACA 0011-64
Incidence at Root . . . . +1 Deg
Incidence at Tip . . . . −1.2 Deg
Aspect Ratio 4.9

HORIZONTAL STABILIZER
Incidence 6 Deg Up, 10 Deg Down

WEIGHT
F-86H-1 AIRPLANES
Full Internal Load and Pilot,
No External Load (Approximate)   18,550 Lb
With Two 200-gallon Drop Tanks
Plus Two EX-10 Bombs   23,700 Lb

F-86H-5 AND SUBSEQUENT AIRPLANES
Full Internal Load and Pilot,
No External Load (Approximate)   18,700 Lb
With Two 200-gallon Drop Tanks
Plus Two EX-10 Bombs   23,850 Lb

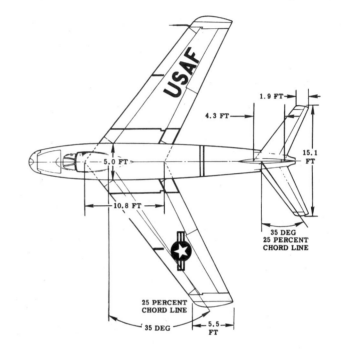

AREAS
Wing (Total) . . . . 313.3 Sq Ft
Ailerons (Each) . . . . 15.9 Sq Ft
Flaps (Each) . . . . 16.3 Sq Ft
Horizontal Stabilizer (Total) . . . . . . 47.2 Sq Ft
Elevators (Both) . . . . 11.3 Sq Ft
Fin . . . . 32.2 Sq Ft
Rudder (Including Tab) . . . . 4.7 Sq Ft
Rudder Trim Tab . . . . 0.6 Sq Ft
Speed Brakes (Effective Frontal Area) . . 9.7 Sq Ft

NOTE For airplanes equipped with slatted extended leading edge wings, increase weight 200 pounds.

● These gross weights are average values. For gross weight of a particular airplane, refer to Handbook of Weight and Balance Data, T.O. 1-1B-40, assigned to airplane.

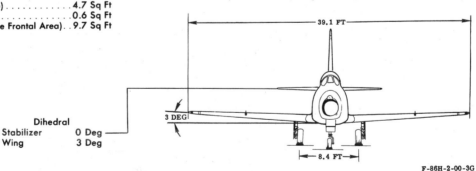

Dihedral
Stabilizer   0 Deg
Wing   3 Deg

F-86H-2-00-3G

Figure 1-10. Airplane Dimensions

Revised 14 February 1958

Reference drawings and measurements of the F-86H.

SIGNIFICANT DATES

22 NOVEMBER 1944
North American Aviation initiates a design study for a straight-wing jet fighter proposal for U.S. Army Air Force.

27 DECEMBER 1944
Letter Contract from Navy Department authorizing the NA-134/XFJ-1 Navy jet fighter.

18 MAY 1945
Letter Contract from U.S. Army Air Force authorizing three NA-140/XP-86 jet fighters.

20 JUNE 1945
XP-86 mock-up approved.

1 NOVEMBER 1945
AAF approval of the North American proposal to change the wing of the XP-86 from a straight leading edge to a swept leading edge design.

28 FEBRUARY 1946
XP-86 cockpit mock-up is approved.

20 JUNE 1946
Fixed Price Contract W33-038-ac-11114 for building of three XP-86 aircraft is approved.

8 AUGUST 1947
XP-86 prototype, #45-59597, is rolled out at Inglewood.

14 AUGUST 1947
689 Board approves the XP-86 prototype.

1 OCTOBER 1947
XP-86 first flight, with George "Wheaties" Welch as pilot.

16 OCTOBER 1947
Fixed Price Contract, W33-038-ac-16013, authorizing production of 33 P-86A aircraft is approved. Later the same day comes authorization for 190 NA-157/P-86B aircraft.

1 DECEMBER 1947
P-86B cancelled. North American proposes fulfilling contract with 188 additional P-86As, plus two P-93A aircraft.

16 DECEMBER 1947
USAF accepts North American proposal to change contract from 33 P-86As to 221 P-86As and two P-93As.

26 APRIL 1948
XP-86 number one prototype officially exceeds Mach One.

15 MAY 1948
Rollout of P-86A.

20 MAY 1948
P-86A first flight.

JUNE 1948
USAF changes Pursuit aircraft designation to F for Fighter, thus the P-86 becomes the F-86.

11 JUNE 1948
USAF awards contract for additional 333 F-86A-5s.

15 SEPTEMBER 1948
Maj. Richard L. Johnson sets World Speed Record of 670.981 MPH in F-86A #47-611.

15 FEBRUARY 1949
94th Fighter Squadron at March AFB becomes first USAF unit operational in F-86As.

MARCH 1949
North American F-86 aircraft name changed from Silver Charger to Sabre.

1 JUNE 1949
F-95A (YF-86D) mock-up is started.

15 NOVEMBER 1949
Letter Contract for 111 NA-170/F-86E aircraft is issued.

24 JANUARY 1950
YF-93A first flight.

11 FEBRUARY 1950
Major Frank Everest sets unofficial world speed record of 710 MPH in an F-86A, Dayton, Ohio, to Washington, D.C.

25 JUNE 1950
Outbreak of the Korean War.

31 JULY 1950
Letter Contract for 360 NA-172/F-86F aircraft is issued.

23 SEPTEMBER 1950
F-86E first flight.

1 NOVEMBER 1950
MiG-15s enter Korean combat.

8 NOVEMBER 1950
First all-jet air battle in history results in Lt. Russell Brown, flying a Lockheed F-80C, shooting down the first MiG-15 in Korea.

9 NOVEMBER 1950
4th Fighter Interceptor Group deploys to Korean Theater of Operations.

13 DECEMBER 1950
Detachment A, 4th FIG deploys to Kimpo AB, near Seoul, Korea.

17 DECEMBER 1950
Lt. Col. Bruce Hinton scores first MiG kill for Sabres in Korea.

19 JANUARY 1951
Letter Contract for two NA-180/YF-100 aircraft is issued.

16 MARCH 1951
Letter Contract for 180 NA-187/F-86H aircraft is issued.

2 APRIL 1951
Letter Contract for 350 F-86A-5 aircraft to be updated to F-86A-7 specifications.

MAY 1951
First F-86Es enter USAF service with 33rd FIG.

20 MAY 1951
Capt. James J. Jabara becomes first all-jet ace in history.

JULY 1951
First F-86Es are sent to Korea.

17 AUGUST 1951
F-86E sets new World Speed Record for 100KM course at 635.685 MPH.

27 AUGUST 1951
81st FIG deploys to England in F-86As, the first USAF unit based in England since the end of WWII.

OCTOBER 1951
Two F-86As converted in Japan to RF-86As Honeybucket photo recon aircraft.

19 MARCH 1952
F-86F first flight.

27 MARCH 1952
First production F-86Fs come off Columbus assembly line.

AUGUST 1952
The "6-3 wing" is tested on F-86F for the first time.

9 MAY 1953
YF-86H first flight.

18 MAY 1953
Capt. Joseph P. McConnell becomes first triple jet ace and top scorer in Korea with 16 MiG kills.

Also, Jackie Cochran sets new Women,s World Speed Record for 100km course at 652.337 MPH.

25 MAY 1953
YF-100A Super Sabre first flight.

21 JULY 1953
First Canadair Sabre Mk 5 comes off the assembly line.

27 JULY 1953
End of Korean War. Final score 792 MiGs shot down against 78 F-86s lost—a 10-1 kill ratio.

NOVEMBER 1953
First F-86As enter service with Air National Guard.

28 OCTOBER 1954
Letter Contract for 215 NA-227 F-86F-40 aircraft is issued.

9 OCTOBER 1958
Last Canadair Sabre Mk 6 off the assembly line.

1 OCTOBER 1961
Two Massachusetts and one New York F-86H squadrons are activated and deployed to Europe during Berlin Crisis.

13 MAY 1968
104th TFS Maryland ANG F-86Hs are activated for duty during Pueblo Crisis.

30 SEPTEMBER 1970
138th TFS/New York ANG phases out the last F-86Hs in service.